Happy Birthday Day
'80th'
Enjoy reading
All my love Brenda xx

C000147960

Keith Skipper's
CONFESSIONS
OF A
NORFOLK
SQUIT MERCHANT

*Curtain calls for
homely humour*

HALSGROVE

First published in Great Britain in 2008

British Library Cataloguing-in-Publication Data
A CIP record for this title is available from the British Library

ISBN 978 1 84114 832 8

HALSGROVE
Halsgrove House
Ryelands Industrial Estate
Bagley Road, Wellington
Somerset TA21 9PZ
Tel: 01823 653777
Fax: 01823 216796
email: sales@halsgrove.com
website: www.halsgrove.com

Printed in Great Britain by
The Cromwell Press Ltd, Trowbridge

Contents

Prologue 5

Early Signs 7

Best Pictures 11

Opening Time 14

Old Barney 18

Panto Fun 22

Mardler Fred 28

Dear Don 32

Pier Launch 35

On the Road 39

"Keep It In!" 44

Major Talent 47

The Aristosquits 50

Key Influence 54

Anniversary Tribute 59

Kipper Culture 63

Homely Band 67

Current Crop 73

Art And Doc 79

Dwile Smile 83

Golden Era 85

Calling Cards 89

Local Olympics 92

Rumlot O' Squit 95

Scary Squit 98

Sparring Partners 101

Grey Power 104

Misery Month 108

Jam Session 112

Sands of Time 116

Crowning Touch 120

Epilogue 125

You never know who you might bump into on these rural rounds. An artist's model by the roadside calls for attention during a scarecrow weekend at Wood Norton. I opened the event and attended to every damsel in distress.

Those who are always right soon find themselves left.

Prologue

I arrived on Saturday, March 11th, 1944, fifth of ten children born to Victor George and Elsie May Skipper at Holmdene Cottages in the mid-Norfolk village of Beeston. Dad was a farmworker. Mum found plenty to keep her busy indoors.

A few days before my birth, tests in Bath – the place, presumably, rather than the overworked tin utensil in our humble abode – on 3,361 children allegedly proved that babies conceived in winter became more intelligent.

I never fully recovered from that shock news.

You know you are getting older when you try to straighten out the wrinkles in your socks and discover you're not wearing any.

Ready to lead the Press Gang troops on a final squit circuit.

Punctuality is the art of guessing how late the other person will be.

1
Early Signs

This is my fourth volume dedicated exclusively to the glories of Norfolk squit – but the first to pay full tribute to what it has done for me since it became clear I would stay in my native county to perfect joined-up writing, cast-off thinking and made-to-measure mardling.

There are still those who consider it inconceivable that anyone claiming to be part of a modern media world rattling along the international information super-highway should be stuck down a country lane exchanging droll yarns, dialect phrases and dogmatic views.

But that's the beauty of Norfolk. It allows a parochial renegade not only the right to exist with impunity but also to flourish without embarrassment in a climate where "dew diffrunt" sunshine regularly breaks through the clouds of dull uniformity.

I became the first boy in our village to pass the 11-plus examination and so head for grammar school in 1955. That's where burgeoning joined-up writing and torkin' proper came in handy, although efforts to sabotage end-of-term reports with small additions in pencil like "intellerjent" and "eweneek" didn't really fool my parents. They looked at paltry marks for most subjects and learnt other new words (spelt correctly) such as "frivolous", "indolent", "disruptive" and "recalcitrant".

It wasn't my fault that most of the cloak-and-swagger brigade with "Cantab" and "Oxon" after their names didn't fully appreciate the educational value of wholesome Norfolk squit. Surely a revelation that "wood comes from trees and many of these are to be found in Canada" and a suggestion that "Chaucer got hold of the Pardoner's Tale when it hung out of the back of his leather

Definition of a dentist - a collector of old magazines.

Apprentice Squit Merchant.

tunic" deserved more than a row of red exclamation marks and an invitation to see Sir in the staffroom long after my train had left the inkpots of Swaffham.

Thankfully, a few shrewd observers of the post-war Norfolk blackboard could see beyond rustic graffiti at the bottom, preferring instead to anticipate colourful and meaningful lines near the top. I was given a bench to reach higher academic marks by headmaster Major I E N Besley, history master Geoffrey Dimock and English teacher Tony Adams.

They put their reputations on the line by organising a "probation period" for me in the VI form. I was stunned and grateful enough to work enthusiastically for two years on Advanced and Scholarship courses. Distinctions in English and a comfortable passage through History set me up for a life in the media.

In fact, I flirted with several other callings before writing to the Norfolk News Company for a cub reporter's job in the summer of 1962. Love of books pushed me strongly towards becoming a librarian. Love of showing off hinted at attempts to get into acting school. Love of mucking about – I hadn't totally forsaken the art – led me to confuse the careers officer who called to smooth our paths into the big wide world:

"What's your name?"

"Skipper"

"Join the Navy. Can you swim?"

"Why? Haven't they got any ships?"

How do you know when you have run out of invisible ink?

I stayed on dry land and collected a "foreign posting" to Thetford to start an extinguished provincial newspaper stint. I soon realised that a sense of humour was imperative to survive.

My farewell salute from Hamond's Grammar School in Swaffham was a copy of Inspector J Daniel Devlin's laugh-a-fortnight best-seller *Criminal Courts and Procedure*. My old custodians were clearly hedging their bets. The book would come in mighty useful for conducting my own defence – or in covering cases for the local press. I had a clear choice.

Always a fearless traveller, I took in the fleshpots of Thetford, East Dereham, Great Yarmouth and Norwich during a 17-year newspaper career. I became most adept at cadging lifts with photographers, magistrates, policemen, defendants, firemen, farmers, doctors, vicars, mayors, cricketers, footballers, councillors and anyone else going towards potential sources of news intelligence. In many cases, they couldn't start without me and I soon began to appreciate how many people simply loved seeing their names and comments in print. "Hold the front page!" turned into my regular ticket to ride.

I survived without a driving licence – the boast persists to this day after a series or reasonably conclusive test failures in the 1980s – and also managed to get by without sitting a single shorthand exam. Imagine, then, my utter surprise when our newspaper training officer Ralph Gray, who doubled as military correspondent, rang me at Yarmouth in the mid-1960s to pass on congratulations for an "outstanding" result. I didn't have the courage to tell him "outstanding" in this case meant Skipper had yet to strike up any kind of relationship with Mr Pitman...

Yes, I had to moderate my penchant for squit at certain times and in certain places – like during earnest debates in the council chamber or at school prizegivings when sensible behaviour was demanded of all in the hall – but there remained plenty of scope for putting a smile on busy reporting rounds.

Faith will never die as long as colour seed catalogues are printed

SMOOTH REPLY

Wife – "Henry, do you realise that you have forgotten this is my birthday?"

Husband – "Yes, dearie, I did forget, and it's quite natural that I should. There really isn't anything about you to remind me that you are a day older than you were a year ago."

I joined in golden wedding celebrations with a few Norfolk yarns, mainly after a second glass of home-made rhubarb wine, and even helped out at annual dinners or meetings when the speaker failed to turn up. The notoriously sharp winter of 1963 brought several unscheduled invitations to mardle at functions where attendances were seriously affected by snow and frost. Confessions of a Country Boy (embellished) filled a few gaps and paved the way towards long service as after-dinner speaker and entertainer on the local circuit.

It seemed quite logical to take my twin loves of writing and talking into another domain when full-time newspaper adventures ended in 1979, although it was a complete coincidence that the BBC should set up a local wireless station only a few months later. I was a founder member of Radio Norfolk, thus finding another constant platform for homespun views laced with squit.

I went back to that 11-plus exam at Beeston Primary School for a rich source of inspiration. I wrote an essay on "My Favourite Radio Programme", picking *Educating Archie* as an easy winner. Well, where else could you find a ventriloquist and dummy on the wireless and not see any lips move?

Here we were, 35 years later, ready to build on that remarkable legacy of the imagination. I rehearsed an opening line.... "and for those listening in stereo, I'm the one in the middle."

Sign in optician's window - "If you don't see what you want, you've come to the right place".

2

Best Pictures

I was brought up on the wireless. Well, space could be at a premium in the small farm cottage I shared with nine brothers and sisters and my parents in the middle of Norfolk during an era when big families were still fashionable.

The Devil's Gallop signature tune sent me into nightly raptures as it heralded the arrival of Dick Barton, Special Agent, ready for more stirring adventures with sidekicks Snowy and Jock. Then came the more lyrical Coronation Scot strains to introduce suave investigator Paul Temple to the platform of rich imagination.

My dear old Nanna, who was blind, kept telling me that the best pictures were on the wireless. Dick Barton and countless others

Taking the mike... Ready for broadcasting duties when
BBC Radio Norfolk opened in September, 1980.

Ideas are very much like children - your own are wonderful.

11

backed her sound judgement over the years, and I regularly vote the 1950s a golden era of broadcasting designed to create an enduring passion for characters of real substance in entertainment and sport.

I adored comedy on the wireless with Arthur Askey, Ted Ray, Jimmy Edwards and Vic Oliver among my early favourites. John Arlott, poetic voice of summer with a gentle Hampshire burr, fed my cricket dreams long before I broke into double figures. Raymond Glendenning, his excitable commentary topping the noisiest crowd, inspired many a thrilling comeback from 10-0 down on the makeshift orchard pitch with jackets as goalposts and the walnut tree our best defender. I still prefer sport on the radio, especially cricket at Test Match time.

So, you'll gather my credentials were difficult to ignore when it came to assembling a team to launch the 21st local station on the BBC map. While most of the others came with considerable broadcasting experience in other parts of the country, I was useful in pointing them towards Carrow Road, Swardeston Cricket Club, Swaffham Market Place, the odd pub in Dereham and a good chip stall in Yarmouth. They were better technicians, but my local

Skipper's boat has run aground on the Norfolk coast

Happiness is a half-way station between too little and too much.

knowledge – and obvious passion for the airwaves – meant a good reception as we got down to business in April, 1980. Less than six months to lift-off. London beckoned to smooth over a few of those rough edges.

Mike Chaney, Radio Norfolk's avuncular boss when the station first went on air.

Knobs, buttons, switches, faders, wires, tapes, microphones... what an introduction to the stereo desk on the first day of our training course in the capital. As I sat trembling at the mysteries of the Mighty Wurlitzer, ignoring yells from insensitive colleagues to talk my way out of that one, ole bewty, a kindly instructor patted me consolingly: "Don't worry, just relax and treat it just the same as you would sitting at the wheel of your car." I had to own up. "But I can't drive a car...!"

He gazed at the heavens and muttered something about special Norfolk problems being foisted upon him. "Well, you can't be good at everything" I mused, humming the tune from Dick Barton, Special Agent.

Perhaps I should have sent for Paul Temple on our return to Norfolk as I tested the capabilities of a portable tape recorder. For all my frantic pushing and prodding, talking and twiddling, shaking and shoving, not a word would it surrender. Fortunately, Radio Norfolk's avuncular station manager Mike Chaney noticed my plight. His fatherly advice proved invaluable many times thereafter. At least when I remembered to use a microphone and switch the dratted machine on.

It was never like this with a notebook and pencil.

A chip on the shoulder suggests there may be wood higher up.

3

Opening Time

Terry Wogan, that most amiable and enduring of radio person-
alities, presented his blarney-packed morning programme
from Radio Norfolk's studios on our first Monday on air. Wogan
was an inevitable winner – and that impish grin seemed to say:
"Follow that!" as he ate his Norfolk dumpling, signed autographs
and returned to the comparative solemnity of London.

Another coup for the talented troupe from Norfolk Tower was
a heady soccer fixture against the Radio 1 disc jockeys at Carrow
Road. The locals won 7–5 with a little help from the Canary camp.
But the important statistics were over £7000 raised for the
Variety Club and a remarkable gate of 9000 on a Sunday after-
noon when families came out for a spot of old-fashioned fun. I

Blarney time... Terry Wogan presented his national radio programme from Radio
Norfolk's studios on the station's first Monday on air.

Does the name "Pavlov" ring a bell?

Carrow Road team... I joined commentator Roy Waller and producer Rob Bonnet for coverage of Norwich City's home matches.

failed a late fitness test. A few weary colleagues must have wished they had followed suit after the game was over.

Those headline-grabbing events apart, the local radio station soon gave notice of qualities designed to turn a new neighbour into an old friend inside a couple of months. It was emphasised when the team came together in early 1980 that it had been selected for its diverse talents from an application list stretching well past 700. Some of the chosen few were better technicians than others. A handful were blessed with sound local knowledge. One brought commercial radio experience from Scotland. A cosmopolitan crew to capture the changes and character in a predominantly rural area.

Reaction from listeners underlined how Norfolk was ready for its own station, with many of those early supporters anxious to play a part in the output. "Come in and talk about it" was a general invitation. We also built up a strong squad of regular contributors from the man who sized up the timetables at Norwich Bus Station to Roy Waller, who cast a critical eye over Canary fortunes at Carrow Road. I teamed up with him on Saturday afternoons for five seasons as match summariser, leaning on my years as a soccer scribe to find the right words for all occasion.

Initially, there were no strict demarcation lines among the Radio Norfolk team – a horses-for-courses policy became established in the second year – and we worked on a rotating basis. That didn't mean we went round in circles, although I was fairly dizzy after first efforts to click switches and talk at the same time.

A diplomat is a man who thinks twice before he says nothing.

TELLING SIGNS

A few tell-tale signs that you're growing old:
- You can remember when everything was fields
- You get out of breath playing chess
- You can remember cover versions of songs the first time round
- You enjoy hearing about other people's operations
- A fortune-teller offers to read your face
- You have a party – and the neighbours don't even notice
- You and your teeth no longer sleep together
- Your ears are hairier than your head
- Your back goes out more often than you do
- You sit in a rocking chair – and can't get it to go.

The idea was to groom a staff of all-rounders, self-operating with confidence on any of the programmes. Following two weeks with Rob Bonnet on the Lunchtime Programme (the Dinnertime Show came later when I served up the regular menu), I hopped across to newsdesk duty. Some of the places in Iran and Iraq were hard to pronounce, especially for the lucky person sorting out the first bulletin of the day while the rest of the world slumbered.

The Breakfast Programme with John Mountford, already a seasoned performer, and lunchtime session, with local, national and international news spread throughout the day, were ingredients from Monday to Friday. Some listeners couldn't work out how we were functioning, opting out of Radio 2, our "mother ship", at certain times of the day. We got regular complaints about Jimmy Young constantly forgetting to mention Fakenham, Frettenham or Fring. Weekend output was geared to longer hours with regular features like Village Voice, Platform's look at the local entertainment scene and Saturday Special highlighting Norwich City's affairs.

There was some danger of catching a cold in rushing to the aid of the Norfolk public. I recall the man who rang up to say his

Alas, poor Yorlik, I knew him backwards.

Reverting to type... three old newspaper colleagues joined me for a special Bank Holiday programme to roll back the years. Left to right: Yarmouth photographer Les Gould, former Eastern Evening News editor Bob Walker and my old Sports Editor Ted Bell.

father's car had been stolen. His father was in France and the car had been taken to a garage where it had been left. We took full details, cleared with the CID and included the item in an afternoon news bulletin.

Within minutes the man called back. It was all right. He hadn't known about it, but his father had given permission for someone from the garage to take the car. And he had been driving along when Radio Norfolk informed him he was in a stolen vehicle!

It was all sorted out amicably. However, it did emphasise the potency and immediacy of Norfolk's new wireless station.

What's cooking? A bearded novice in the kitchen lifts the lid off a special recipe during the early days of Radio Norfolk .

Have you ever imagined a world without hypothetical situations?

4

Old Barney

Radio Norfolk soon built up an impressive army of experts and enthusiasts to throw extra light on all sorts of topics from collecting antiques and writing your will to breeding tropical fish and getting the best out of your vegetable patch.

Most advice and information was handed out in a cheerful, homely manner although lurid accounts of animals' ailments during the weekend phone-in to a friendly vet might spark reasonable complaints from more sensitive listeners preparing meals. One woman with an incontinent terrier and a tabby with dirty habits tried to get on air every time the lines were opened.

One man did succeed in addressing listeners every Saturday morning for seven years – but he had an official invitation to mull over his pet subject of the traditional Norfolk way of life. Old Barney, self-styled rural correspondent for the new local wireless station, travelled into the city on his trusty old bike. The journey could prove hazardous in bad weather, or after a heavy night at his beloved Datty Duck, the village pub which inspired so much of his material, but he invariably turned up on time.

More an observer of others than a character anxious to talk about himself, he started every broadcast with the same greeting, "Mornin' ter all on yer" and ended each one with those immortal words, "Dew yew keep a'troshin'!" Soaked in rural ways, this straight-talking bachelor retired from work on the land had never strayed from his native village roots. He carried strong views on the way country parts were changing and thus served as a useful social commentator for most of the 1980s.

His broad Norfolk delivery regularly reached thousands of listeners, many of them sampling such delights for the first time.

Don't worry about going thin on top. Fat hair is unhealthy.

One can only wonder what they made of glorious inventions such as "coronearshun milk" coming out of a tin, "helter-skeltzer" tablets fizzing in the glass or the "defective van" checking to see if you had a television licence.

Old Barney – Radio Norfolk's popular rural correspondent

In fact, Old Barney turned into a vibrant example of what you can get away with over the airwaves. Created, paradoxically, in the bar of a London hotel where members of the original Radio Norfolk team relaxed after tough training sessions, he soon became my *alter ego* on home soil. I asked him to express and enhance blatantly parochial views that might have drawn sharp criticism from the BBC hierarchy if presented in a more serious and orthodox style. Old Barney's heady mix of dialect and humour helped push through an important agenda in the battle for Norfolk's soul. He'd probably call that "a lot of ole squit" but there would be a ready wink to suggest he had some idea of what I meant.

I wrote and recorded his Saturday morning reflections on the afternoon or evening before to ensure a topical flavour. On a couple of occasions he mastered sufficient technology to phone in when his bike was stolen or he got a puncture. Scripts from the first two years of his career behind the microphone were transformed into three highly successful volumes, Dew Yew Keep A'Troshin', Down at the Datty Duck and Dunt Fergit Ter Hevver Larf. A cassette was also produced with a selection of his rustic tales. All three books were illustrated by former art teacher Patrick Faux Chadwick, who also made a memorable mark on the local entertainment scene as a singer around the pubs and clubs.

What do gardeners do when they retire?

Chad was a regular for several years on my Dinnertime Show, bringing in a home-made composition to share every Friday.

I still bump into folk who thought Old Barney was a real person, not least because he put over sentiments about the changing face of Norfolk with which they could readily identify. Perhaps that's his lasting legacy, an outspoken ambassador for the old guard trying to protect precious qualities of local life at a time of irrevocable change.

Former art teacher Patrick Faux Chadwick – known as Chad on his pub entertainment rounds – illustrated three volumes of Old Barney's broadcasts

HANDY HINTS

Cricket captain's hints to his team pinned up in a Norfolk village pavilion:

1. Don't practice on opponents' ground before the match starts. This can only give them confidence.
2. Should you hit the ball, run at once. Don't stop to cheer.
3. No batsman is allowed to choose his own bowler.
4. Jackson, when bowling, keep you eye on square-leg.
5. Square-leg, when Jackson's bowling, keep your eye on him.
6. If bowled first ball, pretend you only came out for the fun of it. Then go away and sit by yourself behind the hedge.

Never argue with fools. They drag you down to their level and then beat you with experience.

Late night laughter... veteran broadcaster Brian Matthew appreciates a bit of Norfolk squit during his Radio 2 programme from Norwich Theatre Royal.

Digging for a story – an eager radio reporter does the city rounds to see what's developing.

When is the Last Night of the Proms really going to mean it?

5
Panto Fun

Dick Condon was the Irish showman who turned Norwich Theatre Royal into one of the most successful centres of culture and entertainment in Europe. His generosity of spirit, allied to a shrewd business brain, made him loved and respected well beyond an inner circle of showbusiness friends and colleagues.

I think of him often, recalling the smile, chuckle and instant witticism that marked every meeting. He countered Norfolk squit with his native blarney, daring you to take him on at his natural game and then leading the applause if you scored a useful point.

For all his obvious qualities, there were those who questioned his judgement during the weeks leading up to Christmas, 1982. "Britain's greatest pantomime", as he modestly billed it, was in rehearsal with Kathy Staff and Bernie Clifton leading an impressive cast. Impressive? Well, there was at least one dodgy egg in Mother Goose's nest according to some hard-bitten observers of the showbiz scene. "You'll never crack it" they warned. My big break was a cue for big doubts.

Dick Condon decided Nora Batty, an unlikely sex symbol from television's popular Last of the Summer Wine, needed a Norfolk Compo to make her feel more at home on stage in Norwich. The chosen swain would know one end of a pitchfork from another, tork proper, wear a genuine scruffy look and be reasonably conversant with the mating habits of the ferret.

The West End wasn't exactly brimming over with thespians flaunting such qualifications. I got the nod for the part after convincing them I really had graduated from RADAR – Reepham And District Academy of Rustics. Making my professional debut

Do engine drivers eternally wish they were small boys?

on Thursday, December 16th, 1982, having sought permission to change my proffered "Mummerzet" lines into genuine Norfolk, I rushed from behind the Radio Norfolk Dinnertime Show microphone to relish regular prods from Nora's animated broomstick. Mine was a cameo role – "a walk-off part" as one colleague kindly described it – and so there was plenty of time to watch in admiration from the wings.

Staying power is the key to a successful pantomime. A long run with two, and sometimes three, performances a day can tax the most energetic players. They have to remind themselves the next show must be just as vibrant and fresh for a new audience.

Mother Goose enhanced the Theatre Royal's reputation for top-class seasonal fare. I didn't win an Oscar. The Wonderful Waltzing Waters apparently collected more votes than me. But it

A Norfolk Compo gets to grips with Nora Batty. A touching scene from the Mother Goose pantomime at Norwich Theatre Royal when I made my professional debut.

was a memorable experience as well as a great relief to get through to Saturday, February 12th, 1983 without causing any obvious discomfort to a troupe of true professionals. Dick was largely vindicated and he sent me a thank-you note hoping I had enjoyed "a unique opportunity". I took that to mean it wouldn't turn into a regular number.

Kathy Staff eventually had to accept it was a shrewd career move to play opposite a Norfolk legend. She paid me the supreme compliment of saying I was less wooden than some of the characters she had encountered while playing Doris Luke in the TV soap Crossroads.

Why don't we ever see the headline - "Psychic Wins Lottery"?

I put Norfolk charm in the spotlight as Nora Batty weighs
up her chances as Mother Goose.

I taught her all I knew. She continued to pour her talents into Last of the Summer Wine, a pin-up in curlers, pinny and wrinkled stockings, the Cyd Charisse of Holmfirth, her appeal intensifying with every extra layer she put on to keep the elements and funny little men at bay.

An everlasting box of chocolates, she dared you to guess where the soft centre might be. Very few of us have been close enough to lift the lid and rattle the wrapping.

For that alone, I shall always be grateful to the adventurous Mr Condon.

No-one can ever know for sure what a deserted place looks like.

Talent scout.... well, that was the idea behind dressing up
for a stint at Norwich Theatre Royal

The great thing about inflation is that it makes it possible for
people from all walks of life to live in more expensive
neighbourhoods without even moving.

Ready for the last lap of the Press Gang circuit in 2008.

Pushing the boat out for Norfolk culture on Cromer seafront.

The older a man gets the further he had to walk to school as a boy.

MASK ME ANOTHER

A married couple from Sheringham were invited to a masked Halloween party in West Beckham. They were eagerly looking forward to it, but at the last minute the wife cried off with a headache. Even so, she didn't want to spoil her husband's fun and insisted he went on his own. So he set off for the party in full costume

After lying on the bed for an hour, the wife began to feel better and decided she was well enough to go to the party after all. When she arrived the party was in full swing. She soon spotted her husband but chose to keep her presence a secret from him, something she was able to do as he had no idea what her costume was. Instead, she preferred to watch him, to see how he behaved when he thought she wasn't around.

She watched from afar as he flirted outrageously, kissed and danced with other women. Then she figured it was time to make a move on him herself and without revealing her identity.

Disguising her voice, she sidled up to him and said: "Fancy a breath of fresh air?"

"Reckon I do" he replied, "I know the very place."

And with that, he led her to a car in a dark corner where they made passionate love on the back seat.

Both returned to the party but shortly before the big un-masking at midnight, she slipped home alone, removed her costume and went to bed. Waiting for her husband to come home, she wondered how he would manage to explain his behaviour at the party.

"How was it?" she asked when he finally arrived.

"Oh, you know, I never have a good time when you're not there, my bewty"

"Did you dance?"

"No, not once. In fact when I got there I met a few mates and we went down the Wheatsheaf and played poker all evening."

"Oh, yes" said the wife.

"But I tell you," he continued, "the chap I loaned my costume to reckon he had a rare good time."

How many roads must a man travel down before he admits he's lost?

6

Mardler Fred

A plaque on the wall of his village birthplace describes him as "Noted Norfolk author and storyteller." Thousands of regular listeners to his wireless wanderings still smile and nod approvingly at a more homely label of The Grand Old Mardler.

Fred Wigby was one of the most telling discoveries of my career as host of BBC Radio Norfolk's Dinnertime Show from Cell 33. We met in September, 1982 when he presented sound credentials as the writer of entertaining books about his exploits from the agricultural scene of his Norfolk youth to the high seas as a stoker in the Navy and colourful travels and diverse activities back on dry land. His last job was as senior porter at the Fifers Lane residences for University of East Anglia students.

Those travels round the globe gave twinkling Fred a clear edge over other candidates seeking auditions for the role of resident raconteur, and I was anxious to avoid criticism about being ultra-parochial. Fred agreed to a couple of Tuesdays on trial. Anecdotes, asides, home-grown proverbs and a passionate affair with the microphone added five sparkling years to those two warm-up sessions. Fred became a legend in his own Tuesday dinnertime.

I soon dubbed him The Grand Old Mardler as he turned up with a cavalcade of characters bursting to share their rustic philosophies and funny little ways.... Miss Millie, Master Billy, Dewdrop Higgins (who couldn't see any further than the end of his nose), Jimmy and Caleb, Hezekiah Pilbeam, Old John T, Silas Gathergood and many others from his special scrapbook.

Along with his listeners I had no idea where fiction took over from fact or when Wigby embellishment began and ended. No

Where do they keep the ring at a nudist wedding?

matter. Fred was a natural yarner out to prove that the arts of condensation and political correctness ought to be put out to grass.

Verbal gymnastics had to be coupled with studio gyrations on one memorable occasion when his usual microphone left its

fittings. A switch to the other one simply brought immediate disaster as it came away in his hand and couldn't be coaxed back before our live mardle. So, as it dangled, Fred dangled with it. We chortled through the opening minutes of our regular Tuesday stint before an engineer darted in to restore some level of order.

Grand Old Mardler – Fred Wigby became a legend in his own Tuesday lunchtime.

Radio introduced Fred Wigby to a deserved wider audience as he transferred natural skills as a communicator from the written word to the airwaves. A considerable part of his massive postbag came from way beyond Norfolk's boundaries, especially from fellow old salts. Many letters were marked for the attention of "that good old boy who spins them yarns."

It was in early October, 1988, that I headed for the parish of Wicklewood, near Wymondham, for one of the most delightful moments of my broadcasting career. I was invited to unveil that plaque at Oak Tree Cottage, birthplace of The Grand Old Mardler. Family and friends piled into the renovated cottage to salute an outstanding character. He was in top form and remarked with a smile: "I never thought this would happen when I was running about here with the backside out of my trousers!"

Fred died in 2001 just a few days after his 89th birthday. I bet it didn't take him long to start sharing stories in The Great

Is a champagne hangover the wrath of grapes?

Mardling Room in the Sky.... "I'll never forget it. When was it, now? Ah, yes, that was the time Master Billy's trousers caught fire as he dozed off in church next to the stove....."

Perhaps Fred's earliest recollections from childhood set the pattern for a long life full of adventures, laughs and warm comradeship. Father carried him downstairs under his arm to place him under the front room table with his sisters, extinguishing the oil lamp above. Father opened the back door and disappeared into the inky blackness. Then there were loud detonations from bombs being dropped from Zeppelins which left the children trembling and huddling up closer together.

Mardling mates – Broadland reedcutter Eric Edwards passes on a few tips at How Hill.

Roles reversed – Scot Mike Souter dons Norfolk rustic garb while a Radio Norfolk colleague of the home-grown variety tried on the tartan.

Life is like a shower. One wrong turn and you're in hot water.

Creamy waves at Cromer, a key player in the Norfolk squit saga.

The Singing Postman – still inspiring many a good Norfolk turn.

Don't expect anything original from an echo.

7

Dear Don

Another homespun character destined to fit snugly into Radio Norfolk's popular output was the avuncular Don Shepherd. He became a legend in his own Sunday lunchtime – and praise for his uncluttered style soaked in nostalgia came from well beyond the county boundaries.

No less an august publication than the *New Statesman* paid him this glowing compliment in an article praising local wireless in general and Radio Norfolk in particular in July, 1988;

Don Shepherd, who became a legend in his own Sunday lunchtime.

"Its single most memorable programme is Dad's Favourite Tunes, where music from the 1920s to the 1950s is accompanied by the listeners' letters... irresistible narratives of wartime romances, dance hall seductions and eventual bereavements."

Don relished a bit of banter as colleagues affectionately mimicked his staccato delivery spiced with occasional sighs of frustration at not being able to read a letter easily. "I do wish you would print these long words... that would help no end" he chided while insisting on sharing every epistle exactly as it arrived.

This could lead to priceless moments of inadvertent humour. I collected several gems, including: "Dear Don, May I say what a wonderful programme you present for us older folk. The wife and I always have it on a Sunday ..." and the poignant letter from a

Never go to an auction with a nodding acquaintance.

woman in the west of the county who informed Don that one of his most ardent admirers had died "and she was creamed at Peterborough on Tuesday"

Don had graced the local music scene for several years before his Sunday show brought him wider celebrity. He played with the Billy Duncan Band at the old Lido Ballroom in Norwich from 1949 until 1956 and later joined the newly-formed Chic Applin Trio at the city's Norwood Rooms. There were plenty of other shorter stops along the melody way. Many of Don's regular correspondents were old friends.

He helped make Norwich City Football Club top of the pops in 1972 when they reached Division One for the first time. They

HAVING A BALL

My regular perambulations along Cromer seafront and beyond hatch a myriad of meetings, mardles and magical moments.

Favourite so far this year emerged a few days ago on the miniature golf course near North Lodge Park. An elderly couple on holiday with about half a good hip between them were locked in a struggle for supremacy.

She was a timid prodder. He was a lusty basher. Her ball dribbled forward a matter of inches. His raced past the flag like a tracer bullet. They dissolved in helpless laughter – and bade each other a fond farewell.

She took another seven tentative prods to get respectably close to the target while he went hunting across the Cromer pampas. He waved cheerfully on cornering his quarry and warned his partner to keep an eye on the return effort.

After much deliberation, it rocketed back to roughly where he'd started from. They were reunited in mirth about five minutes later as golden sunshine bathed the green. They hugged and kissed and chortled at the prospect of getting full value out of this round.

I watched and listened without making it too obvious until he conceded the second hole because he'd nothing to put in it. She suggested tactfully they come back tomorrow to pick up the contest.

They helped each other slowly back to the hut to return two clubs and one ball. They chuckled off to tea. I did the same.

We're all self-made. Only the rich will admit it.

went to the head of the local Top 10 with The Canaries, the song written by keen supporters Don and his old mate Johnny Cleveland.

Don's wife Vera – they met while working in a Norwich shoe factory – played a vital role behind the scenes, sorting out bumper postbags and records as well as lending constant support at Forties Club pilgrimages around the county. Vera also proved invaluable when it came to tracking down Don's main prop – his pipe.

I sat in for Don several times towards the end of his reign when illness confined him to barracks and soon realised it was unwise, even dangerous, to tamper with a tried and trusted format. If listeners asked for The Old Rugged Cross, One Day At A Time and When Your Old Wedding Ring Was New by the sackful every week, it was politic to play them. The phones didn't stop ringing after the show one Sunday when I suggested it was time to give The Old Rugged Cross a bit of a rest.

Don died peacefully in his sleep at the age of 63 in April, 1991. His funeral service at Heartsease Lane Methodist Church began and ended with Swinging Shepherd Blues, the instantly recognised signature tune for Dad's Favourite Tunes.

A few weeks later a Rum Function was staged in Norwich as a warm tribute to a charming colleague and friend and to raise funds for his widow. Johnny Cleveland was the organising spirit behind this event.

Dear Don's droll sense of humour – "squit with the brake on" I once dubbed it – often emerged from unlikely settings. My favourite concerns him peering out of the window of a village hall as the sun set on a field of stubble after harvest.

Don turned to his musical colleagues, drew out his faithful pipe, tapped it and quietly intoned:

"All is safely gathered in, ere the winter gigs begin."

**What do acupuncturists do when they get an
attack of pins and needles?**

8
Pier Launch

My cheerful relationship with Dick Condon sparked another bold move along the squit trail in the summer of 1984.

The Irish charmer, who had set me up for pantomime fun at Norwich Theatre Royal, followed soon after with an invitation to organise and compere BBC Radio Norfolk's Night of Squit at the end of Cromer Pier, another spot where the Condon magic was weaving its spell.

A full house of over 400 in the Pavilion Theatre roared support for a cast of homespun performers who had become firm favourites on the local wireless. John Crisp had sniffed national pop chart fame with his record Farmer on a Bike. Pub entertainer

"It's a deal". Irish charmer Dick Condon lines up the Norfolk Night of Squit on Cromer Pier... starting point for the great adventure.

You're not going to get anywhere if you think you're already there.

Bobby Benton enjoyed success with his delightful song about the honeycart. David "Muck Carter" Lambert told Norfolk yarns in a wonderfully deadpan style. Olly Day mixed magic and songs. Mawther Maggie wrote her own local verses. Chad warbled in his own endearing style. Major Egbert Gladstone-Pyle of Wanglingham Hall provided a dash of culture.

Naturally, regular listeners to the comparatively new radio station and lovers of our local dialect were out in force, but there might have been several sampling parochial delights for the very first time. There were moments of honest earthy vulgarity – some Norfolk yarns can't live without it – but all performers knew where to draw the line.

This proved to be one of the most significant events of my career. Dick Condon had thrown out a typically chirpy challenge... "I think this squit will sell." He put Norfolk's gloriously understated sense of humour on the same stage as his native blarney. It wasn't a question of which was the better, simply acceptance by a shrewd operator that both could "put bums on seats."

I didn't need Dick to offer a suggestion after our successful Cromer production that squit might be a good traveller around the county and occasionally beyond. But he felt obliged to nourish a sudden burst of enterprise: "I think you could make squit the antidote to Saturday night television" turned out to be one of the sharpest and most prophetic lines from the Condon collection.

It seemed only right to go back to the end of Cromer Pier in October, 2008, to pay homage to our Irish inspiration as the curtain fell on 25 fun-packed years in village, town and city.

Yes, that Norfolk Night of Squit in June, 1984 – a month that saw England's footballers win in Brazil and my old cricket colleagues at Caister lift the Yarmouth Coronation Cup – launched a quarter of a century of travelling entertainment. My troupe of entertainers, gradually evolving into the Press Gang as demands increased and fixtures multiplied, matured nicely together to

If a book about failure doesn't sell, is it a success?

form a mean, green machine, recycling the sort of material which used to fill village meeting places before that blinking box in the corner ruled so many lives.

Olly Day

Magic and songs – Olly Day was in the cast for a Norfolk Night of Squit on Cromer Pier in 1984.

Another key pointer to a busy future on stage came at Cinema City in Norwich in October, 1985. I hosted a Norfolk Night as the radio station's contribution to the Norwich Triennial Festival Fringe. It drew acclaim from audience and press alike.

More Radio Norfolk favourites made their mark. David Woodward appeared as Parson James Woodforde of Weston Longville with slices of life from his famous diary from Georgian times. Methodist minister Colin Riches showed how Norfolk dialect could bring new colour and meaning to favourite Bible stories. Schoolmaster Brian Patrick presented local tales and poems. Mawther Maggie saluted another dialect legend, Ida Fenn, while Mik Godfrey, the Bard of Bodham, offered two stirring examples of the Boy John's memorable dialect letters to the Eastern Daily Press.

A large and enthusiastic audience included Timothy Colman, Lord Lieutenant of Norfolk. I received several requests for more evenings featuring similar salutes to local writers and characters. In many ways, this city event laid foundations for productions of All Preachers Great and Small in Norfolk churches as well as encouraging me to line up more home-grown casts to do the rounds.

Artificial intelligence is no match for natural stupidity.

JUST LOIKE HIS MOTHER USETER DEW

Our George got married wun foin day
Tew his childhood sweetheart Sue
He thowt that she'd look arter him
Just loike his mother useter dew.

They went on honeymoon ter Clacton
And hed a luvly weekend fer tew
But he wuz glad ter git hoom agin
Just loike his mother useter dew.

Fer Sunday dinner, young Sue arst him
Wot he'd loike har tew dew
"Oh, sum good roost beef an' luvly greavy
Just loike moy mother useter dew.

When he cum in from the gardin
He sed ter let the teapot brew
On the kitchen reange for a whoile
Just loike his mother useter dew.

On Monday he arst har furra tea
O' tearters and rich beef stew
And he towld good Sue ter cook it
Just loike his mother useter dew

But she mearde him a ginger pudden
She thowt he'd enjoy suffin new
But thet wuz tanned aside fer thet woont cooked
Just loike his mother useter dew

When he left har luvly pudden
Har anger jest grew an' grew
An' she gi' him a good hard clip o' the lug
Just loike his mother useter dew.

"Now yew look heer," she towld him
"I're had enuff o'yew.
Yew eet that ginger pudden up
Just loike I'm a tellin' yew tew.

An' George...?..he smoiled an' sed
"Ah, good ole Sue, yew'll dew.
I'm glad yew spook ter me loike that
Thass just loike mother useter dew!"

Is a nudist camp a place where nothing goes on?

9

On the Road

It soon became apparent that proper Norfolk culture could fill all kinds of venue from tiny village hall to Norwich Theatre Royal. Demand remained constant even as we decided to make 2008 our last year on the road.

The unashamedly old-fashioned flavour of our concerts attracted big gatherings and regular bouquets, especially in rural parts where the village social used to be at the heart of local life.

Folk who might not have been to their village

Toff of Toftwood in full cry. Comedian Colin Burleigh shows his true colours on stage.

hall or community centre for years told me how much these Norfolk sessions reminded them of home-made efforts both before and after the second world war. "And during it!" emphasised one village veteran.

I was weaned on such delights, a Nissen hut on the old aerodrome our palace of varieties in my home parish of Beeston. I heard wonderful echoes many times as Press Gang perambulations gathered pace.

We twice visited Beeston for shows in the village hall I had the pleasure of opening and also staged productions in nearby communities of Longham, Litcham, Mileham, Brisley and Wendling. Our second Beeston safari coincided with a determined campaign to keep their local post office open. I sent out a clarion call on stage to make the fight count. Lo and behold, Beeston became one

Is "tired old cliché" one?

of the few places to hang on to this vital service while others perished.

Rolling back the years often continued long after final yarns and choruses had faded into the night. Old friends with special memories to share kept on mardling while chairs were stacked, floors swept and farewells exchanged. "I've got a good one for you..." was also a regular prelude to late departure.

We got used to being close to our audiences, especially in smal-

The ideal vehicle for transporting Norfolk squit!

ler venues. I recall a group of cheerful women sitting virtually on stage with the cast at Hanworth, near Cromer, as a late surge packed out the little hall in service since the first world war.

I made a point of writing to thank our hosts after each perform-ance. Many replied with enthusiastic comments along with the amount they had made for their special cause. My favourite response read: "Our village hall has now been listed as a haven for Norfolk squit."

We helped raise thousands of pounds for village halls, churches, schools and other important local facilities. We raised a few thousand laughs as well to underline the sheer joy of live resist-ance to an era of push-button entertain-ment.

Talented all-rounder Greg "Telegraph" Powles.

We never patronised audiences. "Hands up all those bred and born in

Norfolk....right, you can act as missionaries and interpreters for the next three hours." The ideal ice-breaker at a gathering with plenty of "furriners" on show.

Of course, there were "posh" sessions as well, including our parade on a country house stage at Wolterton Hall, near Aylsham, and festival invitations to Dereham, Diss, Downham, Gorleston, Hingham, Mundesley, Norwich and Yarmouth. Squit went international when we put on a show for the Cromer Twinning Association. Three rousing Squit on the Pier productions raised nearly £17,000 for Sheringham-based charity BREAK.

Boy Jimma and Gal Liza sample the high life at Wolterton Hall.

Squit in the City at Norwich Playhouse and the Maddermarket Theatre also pulled in full houses after a successful run of Norfolk'n'Good extravaganzas with old friend Sid Kipper set the standard at the Theatre Royal.

Fixture lists lengthened consider-

Tony Hall – cartoonist, musician and Norfolk legend.

ably as my happy band of troubadours turned into the Press Gang in the mid-1990s. We came under the umbrella of the Eastern Daily Press, my old employers, inviting reporters to join us on stage when we visited their patch.

Then we adopted the EDP We Care Appeal as our regular charity and travels featured healthy bucket collections for that

Would a stitch in time have confused Einstein?

Norfolk Fairy – Sheilah Olley casts her spell on Press Gang outings.

cause. Appeal chairman Paddy Seligman and her colleagues were often on hand to spread the word. Indeed, Paddy attended so many shows we made her official stand-in for any regular unable to appear!

There were a few changes in personnel over the years but the team ethic remained paramount and objectives unchanged – to preach the local gospel with pride and passion.

We embarked on the First Farewell Tour in 2005, realising the need to take serious stock before committing to more hectic rounds from early March until late October. Eventually it was agreed to go out on a high, still on many wanted lists, rather than taper off apologetically.

In any event, a quarter of a century seemed plenty long enough for such an escapade. A growing temptation to wait for requests for certain jokes provided a definite clue about getting out while you are winning.

Gal Liza – putting the world to rights on her Norfolk rounds.

Can you make holy water by boiling the hell out of it?

42

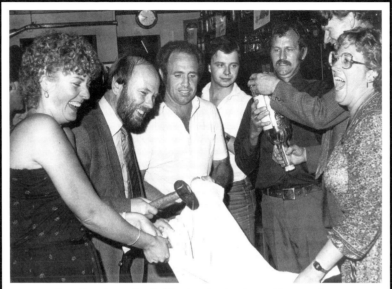

Smashing time – fundraising in a local pub provides a perfect excuse to hit the bottle.

Down on the farm in search of fresh material.

Are part-time bandleaders semi-conductors?

10
"Keep It In!"

Hundreds of Press Gang outings, most of them on the village hall beat, had to bequeath a host of golden memories. An unrehearsed disappearing act – a sort of crash course in squit – emerged as firm favourite on a list of outstanding moments.

I tumbled off the stage at Broome Village Hall, near Bungay, in March, 2001 as my chair wobbled and fell into the well at the side. I was trying to clear the way for a member of the cast to make a move towards the spotlight. A curtain softened the blow, but I had to put up with running gags about "fall guys" for the rest of the evening.

Tony Clarke, at the microphone in the guise of slow-burn comedian the Boy Jimma as the Saturday night drama unfolded, told a full house: "He dunt normally dew that..." Cries of "Keep it in!" greeted my recovery.

Subsequent visits to Broome – yes, they fell for our rustic charms – saw a mattress placed strategically by the stage with a notice warning certain performers not to go too close to the edge.

Occasional guest artist Tony Hall, the Eastern Daily Press cartoonist and talented melodeon player, seemed to attract the worst of the elements. He arrived slightly late at Neatishead Victory Hall looking like a North Sea fisherman lost in a gale, oilskins dripping as he trooped down the aisle to join colleagues on stage. He earned a standing ovation at the end with his Haddock Song.

Tony was about to present the world premiere of his new composition, Bindertwine, at Hingham Village Hall when a torrential downpour drumming on the roof forced a lengthy delay.

Can bishops only move diagonally?

Tuning up for a few more acres of rustic fun with warbler Danny Platton.

There was also the time when his motorbike conked out – and Sheringham Town Crier Tony Nelson rushed to the rescue so he could join us for a show at the Little Theatre.

Tony also seemed to be rather accident prone on stage. His carefully-placed props for a musical rendition would often be sent flying in all directions as he lowered his tall frame into place.

There were several unscripted adventures on the way to shows. A band of cast members got lost in dark lanes around Blo Norton on a stormy night. One performer mistook Aldeburgh (Suffolk) for Aldborough (near Cromer), but arrived before the interval after realising the error of his ways.

Former village headmaster Brian Patrick shared the limelight with his wife Biddy at Aslacton and Great Moulton Coronation Hall. Biddy was evacuated to Aslacton during the second world war and she composed special verses to recall that experience.

Old-fashioned community spirit was never more apparent than on our visit to Hunworth. First, the marquee, which The Bell pub in the village offered to lend, had to be sent away for repairs.

If your ship hasn't come in yet, shouldn't you swim out to it?

Then the organisers had to find a stage and enough chairs from somewhere. The show did go ahead on picturesque Hunworth Green.

The company supplying the pub's marquee stepped in with a replacement. Chairs were drafted in from Bodham and Briston. A stage was built out of potato boxes supplied by the nearby Stody Estate. The pub set up a bar and a local electrician lent his generator for the night.

Boy Jimma came out with another prize line when a light bulb above the stage at Shipdham W I Hall began to flicker dramatically. "Thass like me", he mused, "that come an' go."

Poignancy mixed with humour provided a priceless finale at Longham Village Hall. I was wrapping up proceedings by reminding our audience, which included several close relatives, that there are only three kinds of people in this world – those who can count and those who can't.

A couple of mature ladies near the front looked wistfully at each other. One whispered very loudly: "Oh, dear, that poor boy got that wrong".

USEFUL OPENING

A farmer and his daughter were on their way home with takings from market in pony and trap along a dark, wooded lane.

Suddenly they were set upon highwayman-style and ordered to stand and deliver. The assailant searched them but found nothing, and so satisfied himself by driving off with the pony and trap.

As they trudged disconsolately homeward, the daughter opened her mouth wide and drew out a purse full of gold sovereigns from the sale.

"Here you are, father," she said. "Yew allus did say I hed a big mouth, an' thass cum in handy at larst."

Father threw her a glance and kept on walking.

"Thass a pity yar poor dear mother wunt here. We might he' searved the hoss an' cart!"

The meek shall inherit the earth. Serves them right!

Major Talent

We were returning from another Saturday night of happy homespun entertainment on the Norfolk village circuit.

"There's the obvious title for your memoirs" I beamed while his temperamental old car coughed and wheezed towards the main road. "From the Old Vic to Old Buckenham!"

Peter Whitbread, actor, writer, wit, gentleman and mildly eccentric driver, gave me one of his most enigmatic smiles and turned into Polonius for the next furlong.

Major Egbert Gladstone-Pyle of Wanglingham Hall ready for the high road.

"Though this be madness, yet there is method in't" concluded a master of Shakespeare on reaching a tricky junction with Hamlet by his side. I took the ready quote as generous support for my

Parking is such street sorrow.

suggestion as well as a typically adroit summary of Press Gang antics around local halls and theatres.

Peter often reminded us, without the merest hint of patronising spirit, that the village hall was just as important as the Old Vic. With more than a half century on the professional stage behind him, Peter fitted perfectly into the role of our "cultural icon". He even coaxed his dog Jack into the spotlight for a walk-on, lay-down, wag-tail part in Two Gentlemen of Verona.

Peter died in October, 2004 after a tragic accident close to his home at Briningham, near Holt. We dedicated our 2005 charity curtain-raiser, Squit in the City 2, at Norwich Playhouse to his memory. His long career included several notable Playhouse productions.

He showed me how to mix culture and squit and get meaningful laughs as a result.

We shared a dressing room for the 1982 Christmas pantomime at Norwich Theatre Royal when he played the Wicked Squire and I squared up to Nora Batty as a Norfolk Compo. Peter's pedigree as a classical actor, rubbing greasepaint with the likes of John Gielgud, Paul Scofield and Laurence Olivier, never cramped a sense of fun springing from proud Norfolk roots.

During that Mother Goose panto run we invented a truly outlandish Norfolk character. Major Egbert Gladstone-Pyle of Wanglingham Hall provided a perfect stage for Peter's vibrant imagination, prodigious acting talents and wacky humour. He marched into the wireless studio itching to put the peasants in their place.

It was all off the crisply-turned cuff, one prejudiced outburst after another as he preached the traditional virtues of forelock-tugging, knee-bending and general toadying to the aristocracy. Our inspired radio spoof ran for several years. The monocled major with clipped tones was even invited to open a village garden fete. He appeared on stage to prove Wanglingham really

Silence is not only golden... it's seldom misquoted.

existed. Those able to follow his quick-fire map references would have discovered this fair parish bang in the middle of the Wash.

In more recent years, expertly dovetailed between his highly praised one-man shows, a host of other professional roles and a prolific writing output, Peter became an integral part of the Press Gang. He gave Shakespeare the Norfolk treatment and presented powerful sketches and verses he had penned specially for these outings.

His portrayal of an old man chatting with his departed wife in the village graveyard produced many a gasp and tear in crowded village halls. His eccentric streak could manifest itself in the need to take a quick nap before the show.

He would stretch out on the floor of the stage and fall fast asleep. He always awoke on cue to give another star performance.

Peter Whitbread as St Peter in his highly-praised one-man show, *I Was There.*

Can you cry underwater?

12

The Aristosquits

I grew determined to mark a new millennium with vibrant proof that wholesome Norfolk squit knew no boundaries. Surely it could be just as appealing in a stately home as on a village hall stage...

Wolterton Hall, a handsome Georgian country house built for the Walpoles, seemed the right spot for my grand idea. I wrote to the "great and the good" in the county to find out who would be prepared to do a turn. Lord and Lady Walpole readily agreed to play hosts in the Grand Saloon.

So, on a cloudy but warm evening in July, 2000, The Aristosquits stepped forward for the first time in the name of charity.

Lord and Lady Walpole invite me for a mardle by the moat at Mannington Hall.

Sticker seen on car in Wells - "Spell-checks are hear two stay".

Home Office minister and Norwich South MP Charles Clarke was a late call-off, but three other local MPs played ball, John McGregor (South Norfolk), David Prior (North Norfolk) and Keith Simpson (Mid-Norfolk). Jonathon Peel, Vice Lord Lieutenant of Norfolk, offered serious songs with his wife, Jean at the piano. Anthony Seligman and Tim Ambler saluted Flanagan and Allen while Martin Stiles, Wolterton house custodian, revealed some of the facts behind the Walpole dynasty.

Paddy Seligman – devoted follower of the Press Gang cause.

A full house lapped it up to raise a handsome sum for the Eastern Daily Press We Care Appeal. Chairman Paddy Seligman, ever the good sport, shared compering duties with me amid loud calls to play it again. It was obvious that people more used to cutting ribbons and making formal speeches really enjoyed presenting their party pieces.

Another packed house the following July saw portraits of peers peering down on the latter-day Walpoles again kicking off proceedings with the Lord showing off his Norfolk dialect and his Lady relishing a Pam Ayres poem.

High Sheriff Theresa Courtauld led a light-hearted history lesson while Anglia Television director of broadcasting Bob Ledwidge presented a one-man variety show. The Norfolk expertise in the brutal put-down was demonstrated admirably by South West Norfolk MP Gillian Shephard in funny tales from the hustings when she was "sick of being confused with Edwina Currie".

A "foreign" duo of Lord and Lady Somerleyton from Suffolk acted out comedy songs by American Tom Lehrer which included a spot of cannibalism and a tumbling dress.

The Bishop of Norwich, the Rt Rev Graham James – already a seasoned performer on the amateur stage – donned his episcopal

The day after tomorrow is the third day of the rest of your life.

CONFESSIONS OF A NORFOLK SQUIT MERCHANT

Bishop of Norwich, Rt Rev Graham James, led the company in a sing-song at Wolterton Hall

evening dress to recount amusing anecdotes and lead the entire company in a sing-song about bottle banks.

Judge David Mellor recalled tales from the courtroom, having admitted before curtain up he was "trembling like a jelly" at a performing debut more nerve-wracking than any big trial.

The final act saw Norwich MPs Charles Clarke (yes, he made it this time) and Dr Ian Gibson burst in dressed as policemen to sing The Bold Gendarmes and reel off quick-fire gags at the expense of other guests – including Chief Constable Ken Williams. They told him the pair of them were the increased police numbers coming to Norfolk.

I felt compelled to complete an Aristosquits hat-trick when characters from the local press played prominent roles in the 2003 production at Wolterton Hall. Eastern Daily Press editor Peter Franzen and his deputy James Ruddy stepped out in style with North Norfolk chief reporter Richard Batson.

Lady Enid Ralphs, a sprightly 88-year-old, Norwich prison governor Mick Knight, North Norfolk MP Norman Lamb and my old friend Major Egbert Gladstone-Pyle from Wanglingham Hall were among other turns as the curtain swished down on a remarkably successful run of shows.

"Good to know the upper crust can use their loaf when it comes to squit" emerged as my favourite line as my bright idea took off.

Gillian Shephard, now Baroness Shephard of Northwold, recalled tales from the hustings at an Aristosquits concert.

Clumsiness. Is it catching? Or is it dropping?

All over bar the shouting... a predictable end to the Norfolk squit trail.

Whatever happened to the First of the Mohicans?

13

Key Influence

I never met Sidney Grapes. Yet this colourful Norfolk comedian and chronicler set me up for an all-consuming love affair with our precious dialect and humour.

After making his mark as the archetypical rustic laughter-raiser at local concerts and dinners, the clown prince of Potter Heigham dropped a few lines to the Eastern Daily Press in January, 1946.

The Boy John Letters, all the more eagerly anticipated because they were irregular, continued to delight readers near and far until the author's death on April 28, 1958.

As we marked the 50th anniversary of Sidney's elevation to The Great Norfolk Gathering in the Sky, it was worth reflecting anew on his exceptional flair for combining written and spoken entertainments in such an enduring style.

He was equally at home spinning yarns on stage or creating memorable characters and incidents on paper. Sprinkled with dialect, but never swamped by it, the Boy John Letters were designed to be read out loud – and that's where I served part of my valuable Norfolk apprenticeship.

Family and neighbours warmed to EDP epistles holding up an amusing mirror to village life in those austere years after the second world war. A small but appealing cast headed by Granfar, Aunt Agatha and the cantankerous Ol' Mrs W- reflected many of the daily vagaries we embraced easily on our little patch in the middle of the county.

My emerging reputation as a willing performer, honed on a succession of long recitations at Sunday School anniversaries and a proclivity for impressions of radio cricket commentator John

Television is a weapon of mass distraction.

Arlott while riding my bike, led to requests for public readings of the Boy John Letters.

A few disparaging comments about "squit merchants" and "young hellions what orter be a'larnin' how ter tork proper" did nothing to dull my appetite for a new level of social acceptance.

I even added the latest dialect treat to my Saturday morning party pieces for men building the new council houses just past the old chapel. Pennies and praise took much of the sting out of more mundane chores.

It was in the reading room at Hamond's Grammar School in Swaffham, however, where this pleasure in making a gentle exhibition of myself yielded highest marks in the early stages of a below-average academic career. A fresh Boy John Letter in the paper demanded a genuine swedebasher to do it justice.

Several pupils, most notably those with fathers in the RAF, asked for personal hearings. My stock rose dramatically when I offered rough translations of Norfolk gems like "moderate for the best part o'sum time" and "well, fare yer well, tergether."

This was up there with Chaucer and Shakespeare! That scrawny kid from cowmuck-and-turnip tops land in Beeston had his uses after all despite laughable results in algebra, chemistry, geometry, physics......

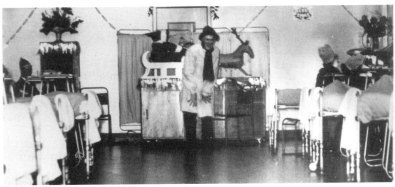

The Boy John spreads some Christmas spirit with his homely squit in a local hospital.

You know what they say - many are cold but few are frozen.

Skipper's Norfolk masterclasses were cut short by the end of the letters delivery service shortly after my 14th birthday, but valuable seeds had been sown. They blossomed into a lifelong passion for a vibrant local vernacular and the Boy John's starring role in keeping it cheerfully relevant on a fast-changing stage.

His vignettes of village life over half a century ago remain full of charm and humour as they saunter along in rhythm with the seasons. Farming and countryside images, particularly from sugar beet and corn harvests, far outnumber boating and holiday snapshots – a real surprise when it's recalled how Sidney Grapes ran a garage at the heart of an emerging Broadland playground.

Perhaps the main characters were based on real people – even the outlandish Ol' Mrs W-, a busybody with more irritating habits than anniversary hats – but Boy John kept topical allusions to the big world outside down to a minimum.

Kindly Aunt Agatha suggested in March, 1952, "We carnt think about Walentines this year, not in these sad times", an obvious reference to the recent death at Sandringham of King George VI.

In March, 1953, Boy John began, "Aunt Agatha sed I dint orter rite one o'my latters wen so many people wus a'sufferen from them terrible floods", and October, 1956, turned a brief spotlight on "that oul Sewerage Canal do."

For the most part, however, we were treated to the latest escapades of a tight-knit community where well-worn traits and tribulations overflowed into knockabout comedy. Most of this stemmed from constant clashes between Granfar and Ol' Mrs W-, protagonists whose antics and utterances allowed no scope for peaceful coexistence, although she nursed unlikely romantic inclinations towards the parochial patriarch.

Aunt Agatha played the genial referee, keeping them apart when tempers boiled and generally offered tea, sympathy and homely advice to anyone in need. Her sound Norfolk credentials were best summed up in this telling extract: "She wus brort up wi'

The less people know, the more stubbornly they know it.

Norfolk comedian Sidney Grapes wore this costume on stage in his role as an old washerwoman. It was sent to me by his niece to find a good home... so I handed it to the Museum of the Broads at Stalham Staithe as a £125,000 appeal was launched to buy the waterside premises for themselves. Patron Henry Cator and chairman Pamela Masters looked on as I rolled back the local entertainment years.

good families an' know how things shud be done. When she go an' keep house up at the farm, she allus tearke orf har earpron afore she anser the phone."

In contrast, Ol' Mrs W- relished a good funeral, a secret tipple and any gossip going. Her introduction in a January letter of 1949 set the tone for countless intrigues to come as Granfar put her in the picture: "She's an ugly woman. Dew you know what? We hed a willage social an' she wun furst prize for the woman who could pull the ugliest face – and she wornt even in the competition."

For me, Ol' Mrs W-'s propensity for mischief, muddle and mayhem reach a peak in the sticky saga of Christmas 1951 when she put a big lump of home-made toffee into her mouth....

"Well, bor, I thort she'd a'chooked harself. Aunt Agatha took har tru inter our scullery, an' them tew managed to git har top an' bottom set, an' the tuffey, orl out in one lump.

"We dint see them for the nex half hour. Ol' Mrs W- she kep apicken orf the tuffey an' eaten on't. She dornt wearst nothen."

That scene of domestic bliss again reduced me to uncontrollable fits of laughter during the recording of a second CD collection of the evergreen letters. I recovered sufficiently to complete this latest tribute to small but beautifully formed slices of local life still lighting up an increasingly grey world.

If you can't be kind, at least have the decency to be vague.

Press Gang stalwarts David Woodward and Brian Patrick – The Back'us Boys.

Pulling a pint after reopening The Ploughshare pub in my home village of Beeston.

Another audition to join the Press Gang ranks.

Do chickens think rubber humans are funny?

14

Anniversary Tribute

To mark the 50th anniversary of the death of Norfolk comedian and scribe Sidney Grapes, I gave the old boy a hand to drop a few timely lines to the Eastern Daily Press editor. The homely epistle was coated in Sidney's beloved dialect and featured most of the characters destined to become household names after his first offering in 1946.

The anniversary letter went with a strong appeal to all readers to "use yar local pust orffice so they can't shut it." As usual, Sidney wrote as he spoke and spelled as he pleased...

Dear Sar,

Reckun you wonder why I hent rit for the best part o'sum time. Well, ter tell yew the truth, I're bin wholly busy a'sortin things out up here what needed attenshun afore they git slung ter one side an fergot abowt. Ole Norfolk habits die hard an yew still hatter be up fearly arly in th'mornin ter ketch me dewin noffin.

Praps I orter bring yew orl up ter date, thow weeks an munths an years dunt mean a site when there ent no calendars an no clocks an no buses and yew kin collect yer penshun when yew feel like it. I go Tharsdys cors there ent no kew and I kin allus cadge a lift hoom wi' sumwun I know.

Aunt Agatha an Granfar, wot live near me, dunt cop the lumbeargo ennymore when they git stuck itter the garden or spring cleanin, an Granfar say he'll be riddy when they need the chimley swept. Ol' Mrs W——hent bin near nor by since Granfar towd har she hed got the ryte sort o'shearpe for a brush.

God only know how that duzzy ole fewl wammed har way inter our little bit o' Norfolk up here, thow Granfar reckun she's only on

I'll never understand metrification even if I live to be a gross.

probearshun for a few hundred year on accownt she're got a ASBO – Actewelly Sorft By Oppointment.

They still dunt git on, Granfar blame har when he git cramp in bed or a tizzicks in his troat an she say thas his folt when har folse teeth ake. They git pletty o' exersize...

They hed a rare set-tew jist arter Easter in 1974, I think that wuz, when she wolunteered ter help him fye out the shud an tricolearte that up fer summer, Blarst me if she dint jam orl over his trays o'best seed tearters an tip a pot o'red pearnt down the wall whot wuz spoozed ter be see-green.

'Boy John'.

He hulled whot wuz left over har smartest anni-warsary hat what she bort at a rummage searle in Ludham arter the war.

There they wuz, both onnem, overcome wi' emulshun while Aunt Agatha moved in ter keep 'em apart.

"A little bit of earth in heaven" say the Wicar, wot got here well afore the rest onus ter make sartan this Kingdom hev got proper Norfolk accents.

Oh, he're got anuther job a'keepin his eye on our ole hoom patch at Potter Heigham an few uther places rownd the Broads jist in cearse we hatter bild a gret ole Ark an hoss that down when the worter start cumin in...

We hed a proper Norfolk git-tergether lasrt week ter mardle about yar globul warmin an the loike. Ted Ellis an John Knowlittle

The human body, with proper care, can last a lifetime.

think that myte he' suffin ter dew wi' orl that hot air cumin owter Natrel England an that there Vyromint Ajency. Dick Bagnall-Oakeley say larst C Level rise he kin remember wuz in clarssrum at that posh Gresham's Skewl when sum bryte kids hatter take jogrophy exam.

Dick's still a'tellin his yarns an mearkin orl on'em larf, speshully that one bowt th'ole chap whot got a lift in a farst motor. "Dew yew allus go that quick?" he arsk the driver. "Why, I go much quicker when I'm by myself" say the young man, showin orff. "Blarst me," say th'ole boy, "I'm suffin glad I dunt travel wi'yew when yew're on yar own!"

Must tell yer, I bumped inter Ida Fenn nut long back – yew know, har woss Fleggmatic bowt most things – an she reckun we're jist gotter keep a'dewin an hope fer the best. She allus did tell'em rown Yarmuff way how that myte be hard gowin arter orl them Scotch fishergals went hoom when the herrin dried up.

Yis, thass suffin nice ter be among yer own. I give 'em bit o'squit now an agin an Granfar's gorter sing "Tom Bowlen" at the next harvest horkey. He'll sing it agin if he git un uncore. Ol' Mrs W—— is tryin ter revive "Kissin in the ring" but I dunt give a site for har charnses while har folse teeth keep darnsin up an down.

So theer y'are, some things dunt chearnge much an they dew tell m thass how Etarnity got started. Us Norfolk lot send owr werry best wishes ter yew, yar staff an orl whot read this here letter.

Fare y'well, tergether an dunt fergit ter celebrearte St Jarge's Day. Yars obediently,

THE BOY JOHN

PS: Aunt Agatha, she say: "Time dew fly –speshully when yew're wi' the angels!"

Marriage is the alliance of two people, one of whom never remembers birthdays while the other never forgets them.

Don't get annoyed if your neighbour plays loud music at two in the morning. Call him at four to say how much you enjoyed it.

THE VICAR AND I WILL BE THERE

Dear Friends, I'm the curate of Slushford-on-Creek,
My name is the Reverend Septimus Meek;
The vicar and I work so hard as a rule,
Today there's a meeting at our infants' school;
And the vicar and I will be there,
For we are an industrious pair.
The mothers, of course, at the meeting will be,
At 20 past two they'll be handing out tea
And a silver collection is taken at three
So the Vicar and I will be there.

I'm awfully sorry for poor Mrs Jones,
They say she has terrible pains in her bones.
She lives all alone and she suffers, I fear.
But tomorrow some friends will be calling, I hear;
And the vicar and I will be there.
For we are an industrious pair.
They will bring her such joy she'll forget all her pain,
With flowers and fruit she'll be quite well again,
And the squire is sending a case of champagne
So the Vicar and I will be there.

Katherine Perkins is our village belle.
I fear me, alas – still, no matter – ah well –
But let us rejoice, for this maiden serene
Will be married tomorrow to Samuel Green
And the vicar and I will be there
For we are an industrious pair.
The bride will look sweet as she walks down the floor
But still in the throng, though the fact she'll ignore,
Will be several fellows who've kissed her before
And the vicar and I will be there.

The town hall next week we have taken, you see
We're giving the wounded some afternoon tea
And Lady Fitzgargle – you heard her before –
Is giving us music from three until four,
And the vicar and I will be there
For we are an industrious pair.
She means very well, but she's hardly a star
And as soon as she sings, and they hear her afar
Quite a lot of those boys will retreat to the bar
And the Vicar and I will be there.

Never use a long word when a diminutive one will do.

15

Kipper Culture

A modest megastar from the parish of St-Just-near-Trunch emerged as Norfolk's leading cultural ambassador of recent times – by breaking most of the rules.

Sid Kipper defied tradition by taking on missionary work way beyond home shores. That meant he was cast for too long as a prophet without real honour on his own midden. He refused to compromise, however, and his potent mixture of squit and culture eventually collected deserved plaudits.

Father Henry and the boy Sid form The Kipper Family to take Norfolk culture on a madcap journey.

He combines singing, storytelling, broadcasting and writing in such seamless fashion it's difficult to know where to fit him on the entertainment scene. Perhaps "talented all-rounder with sideways stance" offers the most useful clue to the skills of a performer behind such classics as Prewd and Prejudice, The Crab Wars, David Kipperfield, The Pied Blowpiper of King's Lynn, Three Gruff Billy Goats, Bunfight at the OK Chorale (set in the old Tame East) and the local vicar's Letters to the Truncheons. Now, what would the Boy John make of those?

Sid takes his distinctive brand of humour all over the country and occasionally abroad to show Norfolk is way ahead of the field when it comes to lateral thinking. Happily, his constant homecomings now attract full rations of adoration.

Does an osteopath work his fingers to your bone?

I have worked with him many times on stage and radio, cheerfully challenging occasions as he steps away from normal thought processes and explores the most unlikely avenues for fresh inspiration. As his fame spread, I suggested he makes a habit of capturing the true spirit of Norfolk, teaching it new tricks and then sending it on its way to run riot across the land.

A regular on BBC Radio Norfolk's zany panel game Should The Team Think?, Sid invariably takes simple subjects to new planes of meaning and mirth. Chairman David Clayton tries to sum it up: "From the first time he opened his mouth on the first programme at Hunstanton Princess Theatre in 1994, I have marvelled at Sid's peculiar and hilarious take on Norfolk life. I assumed I'd get used to him. I don't think I ever have. More to the point, I might stop laughing if I started understanding him."

Sid made his mark on the local folk circuit as part of The Kipper Family, teaming up with father Henry, a born-again defender of the folk tradition who became custodian of his father's collection of old songs. I interviewed them several times as Henry basked in his reputation for having one of the foremost voices in the country.... "but we don't know who might have the other three".

Sid recalls those early days. "Father started to go round singing them old songs and I thought it my duty to go along and help him out. I used to do what they call counter-melody. The idea was to try and counter what Father was doing to the melody by distracting people with some different notes."

The partnership ended in 1991 with a surprise retirement party for Henry. He didn't know he was retiring. Relations between the pair had clearly become strained. "It was the little things" said an observer at the time, "like one of them leaving the room whenever the other came in."

Henry went into an old folkies home. He went on the run and the family lost touch for a few years. Then, just two weeks before his death in 2000, he turned up at the family cottage. Despite the

Is a friend someone who dislikes the same people as you do?

change of locks, he had managed to gain entrance. There they found him, sitting in the old chair by the fire as if nothing had happened.

He was to die peacefully in mid-anecdote. A moving tribute in the Trunch Trumpet, official organ of the Sid Kipper fan club, emphasised: "So, in a very real sense, he went quietly in everyone else's sleep."

Sid Kipper – leading cultural ambassador with a sideways stance.

The funeral was taken by the vicar of St Just, the Rev "Call-me Derek" Bream. He performed a rather modern form of service which included the coffin being placed in the cloakroom according to the laws of feng shui. The congregation stood and clapped their hands over their heads as they movingly sang Another One Bites the Dust.

Sid launched his solo career with a performance in Chichester: "I started singing The Stick of Rhubarb, and right from the start they was with me. What's more, they was still with me at the end, which is always a good sign 'cos sometimes they sneak off if you sing with your eyes closed and you don't notice till there's no applause."

I have long admired Sid as a literary master. His captivating Prewd and Prejudice, first published in 1994, follows a woman leaving polite London society for the depths of rural Norfolk. In 1904 St Just-near-Trunch was only half-civilised... `

Plants grew unchecked, unruly birds woke her before dawn, there was not a milliner for miles and Harrods flatly refused to deliver. From All Idiots' Day to Old Soaks' Day, Miriam Prewd's

If you try to fail and succeed, which have you done?

Festive panellists for BBC Radio Norfolk's Should The Team Think? Sid Kipper, Keith Skipper, Ivan Bailey, Roy Waller and chairman David Clayton.

diary unravels a rich tapestry of country customs. She encounters June Pole Dancing (Norfolk's a bit behind at times), the Pedant's Revolt, the Valentine tradition of exchanging embroidered underwear, the Trans-Norfolk Highway and the ancient monument of Flinthenge. Sid, of course, tries to guide us through the strange goings-on.

Adrian Bell, Sid's long-time publisher at the Mousehold Press in Norwich, remarks: "Underneath his humour with its characteristically Norfolk deadpan delivery and irreverence for figures of authority, there is a seriousness of intent. He is a countryman at heart who remains unimpressed by the bright city lights and the seductions of 'modernisation' and all those other contemporary buzz words.

"Make no mistake – Sid is a very funny man but his wit is shot through with shafts of wisdom. They tell us laughter is good for your mental health. So is Sid Kipper."

A true inspiration and friend, the likely lad from St Just-near-Trunch proudly carries the Norfolk flag to parts others simply do not reach – or even contemplate.

Why are double negatives a complete no-no?

16
Homely Band

Norfolk humour may not dig you in the ribs or smack you in the face. But it can tickle your fancy like no other. Traditional fare based on gentle goading and masterly understatement retains a meaningful role simply because there's always room for the kind alongside the cruel.

This may reek of rampant nostalgia or deluded parochialism to those who prefer their comedy to march with the times, push back boundaries, plunge into embarrassing waters and put a sad and cynical old world in so-called perspective.

Sidney Grapes and a large band of homely disciples may be rooted in time and place but their offerings retain genuine charm and value because they are wholly unpretentious, softly amusing and admirably self-effacing. Okay, not quite at the cutting edge – but still at the warm heart of a cheerful remembrance parade.

I went in search of home-grown performers, some of them neglected, half-forgotten and overlooked, to lure them back into the spotlight for well-deserved bows.

Jim Howard divided much of his time between the roles of deputy head at the old Reepham Secondary Modern School and Farmer Giles spreading unlimited mirth as leader of the Heydon Minstrels.

They entertained in 44 villages. Performers included Jim's wife Sylvia, who played the piano for shows and often wrote topical lines for his Farmer Giles song a few hours before he stepped forward.

Did you hear the one about the American who formed a Norfolk concert party to raise funds for Coronation celebrations? Al Dexter began a recruitment drive to fulfil a long-standing

What do you send a sick florist?

ambition. There were still several American servicemen in Norfolk at the time. Some were billeted at Heydon Hall, that most delightful of mansions built in the 1580s, travelling each day to the airbase at Sculthorpe. "The chain reaction eventually reached me and I became a member of the original cast" reported Jim Howard.

The curtain went up at Heydon in April, 1953. Jim had a solo spot and sang a Gracie Fields number, The Little Pudden Basin. The final chorus of Carolina in the Morning was to become the group's farewell trademark.

Will Judge in his rustic outfit.

Heydon Minstrels hit the village trail that summer, helping to raise funds for countless Coronation jollifications. Then before the start of the 1954 season, Al Dexter was posted back to America and the producer's cloak was tossed to Jim.

For over two decades he slid effortlessly into the parts of organiser and dispenser of rural wit, poking fun at the clergy, teachers and compatriots close to the land. "Not a very difficult task" said Jim, "because the true Norfolk countryman loves nothing so much as a good laugh, even though he may not realise he is laughing at himself."

Do you put on weight if you jog backwards?

THE CANARY DIRECTOR

The Canary director stood at the gate
His head bent very low
Sadly he asked the man of fate
Which way he had to go

"What have you done?" St Peter asked,
"To seek admission here?"
"I was a Canary director, Sir
For many and many a year."

"A Canary director?" the old man mused,
Then he gently pressed a bell,
"You step inside and choose a harp.
You've had your share of hell."

Sam Fowle and Baden Dew were founder members of the Cigarette Concert Party in the early 1930s. In fact, the name of the troupe changed according to which villages they visited. Around the Burnhams, Baden's home patch before he moved to Heacham, they would be known as Baden Dew's Concert Party. If they performed in the Harpley-Massingham area, Sam Fowle's name would be up front.

Sam, an onshore fisherman, sold shellfish from a pony and cart, travelling regularly to West Norfolk villages. He and Baden were busy during the second world war with ENSA concerts at the old Pilot Cinema in King's Lynn where they teamed up with Gerry Myers, billed as Norfolk's answer to Arthur Askey.

Sam was not called up for military service because of his work supplying food. Baden was ruled out by a leg problem. They performed sketches and comedy songs together, one of their most popular numbers starting: "How dew yew dew everybody, how dew yew dew and how are yew?" Then they would name someone in the audience a follow up with a cheeky punchline.

If love is blind, why is lingerie so popular?

Their pianist was George Collison, while others joining them on stage included soprano songbird Madge Boothman, baritone Frank Tyrer and conjurer John Murray Smith, who later turned professional, and Jim Covell, "the Great Covello". They would also invite Ernie Pull, Charlie and Margaret Rand and Eric Meek, collectively known as the Snettisham Hillbillies.

As none of these artists owned cars in those days, anyone who booked them had to arrange transport, usually from bus company Duckers of Hunstanton.

For his day job, Sam Fowle would often leave home at 3am with pony and cart in order to get to outlying villages at a reasonable time – both candle lamps on full power! Peggy the pony knew her way home after the shellfish round, a handy gift as Sam and his brother often nodded off when the last call had been made.

Back in the 1920s, Dereham was at the heart of homespun entertainment. A concert party called the Mountebanks, including the evergreen Banjo Saunders, who was in the line-up for a minstrel show at the Corn Hall in aid of the "deserving poor of the town" on December 7th, 1897.

Harry Lambert formed the Odds and Ends at Dereham in 1925 and they drew packed houses in the Public Hall and surrounding villages. When the group disbanded in 1930, several performers continued to appear in local concerts. Singer Barney Simmons and Mr Faux and his Talks with Chalks were big favourites.

The Odds and Ends came together again to provide entertainment for the troops during the last war. Star turn was Buster Newell, all dressed down in his old smock, red neckerchief and chummy hat and holding forth with stories and songs in the broadest of broad Norfolk. Expressions on the faces of soldiers from "foreign parts" were nearly as funny as Buster's routine. How much of the squit went home was a matter for considerable debate in the bar afterwards.

Never agree with a fool. He may be doing the same thing.

Will Judge changes character dramatically!

Will Judge (1883 – 1960) played a canny border game during a successful music hall career. He was billed as The Original Norfolk Comedian despite being born in Beccles, making his first public appearance there and returning to live in the town after shining as principal comedian on the pantomime stages of London.

Well, where there's a Will, there's a shrewd way of making the most of your local connections. Evidently, Will took a bow at the Lowestoft Hippodrome in 1906 as Suffolk's Own Comedian. He saw fit to put on Norfolk garb and sing that county's praises when his Norwich booking increased.

Will and his wife Gertrude Orchard formed one of the best-loved double acts in the business. His range was impressively wide – villain, simpleton, old crooked man, elegant woman and a saxophone turn to supplement his comic talents.

He was organising his own repertory company in Beccles at 14 and one of his favourite pieces was the dying act of Nelson. "We used to buy fireworks for the show and as I was gasping 'Kiss me, Hardy', giant squibs were bursting over my head" he recalled.

A pessimist is a man who burns all his bridges in front of him.

What a team! Press Gang performers prepare for their final tour at North Walsham Motorcycle Museum.

When geese listen to horror stories, do they get people bumps?

17

Current Crop

I t's so tempting to find a comfortable seat down memory lane, size up a glorious cavalcade from a golden era and sigh with regret that their like will never be seen again...

Well, I've been in a perfect position for many years to claim such notions are misguided when it comes to dispensing wholesome Norfolk squit and wit, either on stage or in print. My roles as writer, broadcaster and entertainer, culminating in proud leadership of the Press Gang performers for a quarter of a century, have underlined not only ample scope for safeguarding a rich legacy but also a healthy desire to build on it.

In many ways, Dick Bagnall-Oakeley was the natural successor to Sidney Grapes, speaking and writing in Norfolk dialect with equal facility. A gifted all-rounder, he taught geography at Gresham's School in Holt and made himself an authority on migrant birds in North Norfolk. He was also an expert on capturing wildlife on film.

Dick's informal and humorous talks, both on local television and at lectures throughout the region, made him a popular figure. He died in 1974 but his fund of Norfolk yarns remain in circulation. He warned: "When you read Norfolk tales, remember that they are tales about a highly observant, subtle and recondite people. Therefore always think twice before you laugh at a Norfolk tale.

"The laugh might be on you!"

David "Muck Carter" Lambert also stayed true to traditional traits on the local comedy circuit, deadpan delivery and rustic garb almost tempting audiences to believe he was a few sticks short of a bundle! Perhaps the biggest tribute to his homely style

A good pun is its own reword.

Stately gathering outside Wolterton Hall before a Press Gang show in one of Norfolk's finest country houses.

is the way his earthy repertoire has been shamelessly purloined by several colleagues still doing the laughter rounds.

Farmer Keith Loads became an integral part of the Thursford Christmas Spectacular, introducing thousands of folk to Norfolk's sense of humour through his annual festive platform. The Nimmo Twins built up a big following, especially in Norwich, with their sketches and observations from the sharper end of the comedy spectrum.

Growing old is mandatory. Growing up is optional.

Several performers of recent times have mixed music with humour, Ollie Day, Winston the Singing Farmer and Nigel "Boy" Syer among them. While some holidaymakers and newcomers may find a strong Norfolk flavour hard to take – I'm sure the Singing Postman caused some confusion along Yarmouth's Golden Mile for a brief spell in the mid-1960s – homespun fun remains enthusiastically welcomed in countless local venues.

It was a privilege to be at the heart of that cordial reception committee in village, town and city with my Press Gang colleagues from 1984. I watched a dedicated crop of squit merchants relish the challenge of spreading our special brand of fun among audiences of all ages and sizes. Naturally, some stints went better than others, but all carried an infectious air of genuine respect for familiar yarns and their targets.

Former newspaper reporter Tony Clarke brought uncanny echoes of the legendary Boy John to our cultural travels. He

On parade in the Grand Saloon at Wolterton Hall... squit goes up-market.

Is it progress if a cannibal uses a knife and fork?

dressed up as Boy Jimma with his trademark smock handed down with family stories and a slow-burn delivery that often threatened to linger way beyond closing time. An endearing habit of interrupting himself and then asking the audience and cast exactly where he had got to in his riveting discourse could add several minutes to his allotted span.

He proved as well how the pen can be just as mighty as the boards when it comes to sharing a cheerful gospel. Two volumes of rustic memoirs coated in dialect, Mighta Bin Wuss and Thass a Rum Ow Job, highlighted country ways fast fading into the sunset.

Tony's madcap scripts for annual off-the-cuff pantomime productions by Friends Of Norfolk Dialect enhanced a glowing reputation for catching the vernacular delightfully in print and on stage.

I dubbed Colin Burleigh the Toff of Toftwood more out of admiration for a snazzy line in waistcoats than for any concessions to sophisticated humour. A man of many parts, some of

Taking his time – Boy Jimma kept quick-fire repartee to a minimum as he tried to keep up with himself.

them tricolated up by heart surgeons at Papworth Hospital, he developed an energetic stand-up act with plenty of saucy touches and a neat line in self deprecation. Scurrilous slices of fiction involving his wife June and his home patch around East

Times flies like an arrow. Fruit flies like a banana.

Dereham gave his routine a topical edge and occasional whiff of scandal.

A long and successful career on the traditional jazz scene as warbler, drummer and show organiser saw Colin bump into countless old friends during Press Gang missions. Interval extensions had to be hastily renegotiated to fit in all those reunions.

Pat Nearney, the Norfolk Nut, relied on a down-to-earth "cheeky chappie" approach to ease his way through material that could have been embarrassing in lesser hands. "That was a little bit naughty, wasn't it?" he asked as customers chortled and called for more. No surprise to find he included a Max Miller tribute in a surprisingly wide repertoire.

Pat honed his comedy instincts on years of writing and appearing in pantomimes at Mundesley. Stand-up bookings in holiday camps and other testing arenas gave him a fearless streak to go with a truly engaging personality. Perhaps those seasons as a football referee helped prepare him for a pitch at becoming one of Norfolk's most popular comedians.

Mik Godfrey developed his droll skills as one of the hosts of Bodham's notorious Nights of Squit in the village hall. (Rehearsals afterwards in the Red Hart pub next door) There were plenty of unplanned gaps to fill

Mik Godfrey, the Bard of Bodham.

Why is there so much month left at the end of the money?

with gentle reflections on familiar characters and incidents culled from the Bard of Bodham's job as a bus driver. He also brought his own distinctive manner to readings of Boy John Letters on Press Gang rounds.

Pat "Mangoldgrinder" Maitland needed a ready sense of humour as a driving instructor over many miles. He could change gear adroitly on stage, steering cheerful fact and fiction round the sharpest bends.

He claimed to have a job for life as he tried to teach me to drive. I called it a day after a series of failed tests – but recalled laughter-loaded lessons when we both passed squit examinations.

Greg "Telegraph" Powles, actor, broadcaster and very tall stand-up comedian, demonstrated commendable daring to experiment while savouring the role of the "Press Gang's youth policy". His one-man version of the balcony scene in Romeo and Juliet with a strong whiff of Norfolk left him as exhausted as those watching as he charged up and down from the stage. He came to grief at Waxham Barn – but picked himself up like a real trooper and carried on regardless.

He passed on that "youth policy" mantle to Robin Skipper on the final laps, my teenage son specialising in his own tribute to the talents and tales of Sid Kipper.

We were blessed with a couple of lively mawthers on parade as well in the diminutive shapes of Elizabeth Austrin (Gal Liza) and Sheilah Olley (Norfolk Fairy). One was voted Miss Broadland Lovely Legs just after the war – and then again in 1922. The other had the power to wave her wand and turn boys into a lay-by just after midnight.

So that vibrant brand of truly local humour, much of it ambling along slowly enough for "furriners" to catch up, continued to cock a snook at passing trends and send a warm glow round hundreds of community meeting places at the end of one millennium and the beginning of another.

Why don't sheep shrink when it rains?

18

Art And Doc

It's time to introduce a brand new Norfolk double-act anxious to dispense rations of native wit and whimsy.

Art and Doc, believed to be cousins from the Morston area and sharing a strong nautical background, have joined forces "to keep the record straight on certain important matters affecting Nelson's county."

They speak with broad local accents but have agreed to be phonetically modified in print in order to reach as wide an audience as possible. Art and Doc are not their real names, but any resemblance to younger and more trendy characters seen on national television is purely unfortunate.

Art claims he's called that because he can draw a pension without taking his pencil off the paper. His partner reckons he's been teetotal since prohibition reached Blakeney and therefore deserves to be called Dry Doc.

They'll deal with topics of local significance in a homely but forthright way.

Their first treatise sheds fresh light on a long-running linguistics debate over the county's most famous son:

Nelson Touch

Art: Do you reckon Nelson spoke with a Norfolk accent?

Doc: Cor, blarst yes! Boy Horry never lost his local twang even though he didn't get home as often as he wanted to.

Art: Not many stagecoach runs to Burnham Thorpe those days from depots around the Nile. Didn't he have a lot of Norfolk lads with him on his travels?

Sign on door to maternity ward - "Push, push, push!"

79

Old salt Art.

Old salt Doc.

Doc: He did, and his own servant Tom Allen was one of those he enlisted from the Burnhams. Tom met King Ferdinand when he came aboard the flagship at Naples and extended a regal hand to be kissed. Well, Tom shook it and said in a broad Norfolk accent: "How d'yer dew, Mr King!"

Art: Very polite. He could have called him "Ferdy, my ole bewty!" and locked him in a half-Nelson. Did Horatio write in the vernacular?

Doc: No, he used vellum like most admirals…

Art: And when scurvy broke out, he had him locked up again…

Doc: Well done, mate! Yes, Boy Horry could write just as proper as he talked. Look at this letter to Lady Hamilton… "Dearest Emma, I git orl of a muckwash just thinkin' 'bowt yar dumplins boilin' over. Keep th'lid on till I cum hoom."

Art: Could be more steamy revelations this year with it being the 200th anniversary of the Battle of Trafalgar and Lord Nelson's death at the moment of his greatest triumph.

Doc: Yes, I've already had a BBC television documentary team asking me what I remember of the lad from Burnham Thorpe.

Why do we wait until a pig is dead to cure it?

Art: What on earth did you tell the cheeky beggars?
Doc: I said he was okay – but I liked his father better.

Coastal Breezes

Art – Those lazy old winds keep coming our way.
Doc – Yes, straight from the Urinals with nothing to stop 'em.
Art – I asked one of those posh newcomers how he found the weather.
Doc – And he said he just went outside and there it was.
Art – Bet the beach didn't come up to his expectations.
Doc – No, but the waves went just past them. He's on the short side.
Art – You told that smart woman with a sou'wester that you lived next door to Morston Harbour.
Doc – Yes, and I invited her to drop in any time she liked.
Art – I do admire the manner in which you seek to ingratiate yourself with trippers.
Doc – Well, they need to be told how Blakeney is so good for bronchitis.
Art – I went there once, and I soon caught it.
Doc – See, good Norfolk advice well worth sharing.
Art – What do you tell strangers who ask where a certain road might go?
Doc – I simply inform them that it goes nowhere – it stays here, where it's wanted.
Art – What's that new leaflet you're holding?
Doc – It's issued by the Norfolk Bridge-Building Society and is called 'Towards Peaceful Co-existence – Hold Your Slarver and Listen!'
Art – Here's to a bumper holiday season.
Doc – And we'll keep taking it in turns to be the village idiot.

Best way to get a youthful figure is to ask a woman her age.

Good Old Days

Art: My parents were so poor the woman over the road gave birth to me.

Doc: That's nothing. We couldn't afford laxatives in our tied cottage so Mother used to sit us on our pots and tell us ghost stories.

Art: I remember how we knocked a hole in the kitchen wall so we could dip our crusts into next door's gravy.

Doc: Huh, my parents couldn't afford shoes for us. They painted our feet black and laced up the toes.

Art: Happy times. Wouldn't have missed 'em for anything. Funny, but Mother was born in Wells, Dad was born in Cley and I was born in Morston. What a remarkable coincidence that we should all get together.

Doc: That's Norfolk fate. We all had our share. I wore hand-me-down clothes for years.

Art: Did that embarrass you?

Doc: Just a little. I had seven sisters.

Art: Still, you ate well when your Aunt Harriet stayed up all night to knit together two pounds of mince so you could have a joint for Sunday dinner.

Doc: We had to make do and mend. Make a lot of a little; Look after each other. Big families in those days.

Art: There were 13 of us. Think I was number eight. Every time the kettle boiled we sent for the midwife.

Doc: So much washing in our kitchen we had a rainbow in the front room.

Art: Didn't your mother invent the first spin drier in Norfolk?

Doc: Dead right! It was a hula hoop with linen pegs.

Art: They really were the good old days

Doc: With the three R's to remind us .....

Art: Rickets! Ringworm! And Ration books!

Never believe anything until it is officially denied.

19

Dwile Smile

Anthony Grey composed himself. A world premiere with the accent firmly on Norfolk demanded full-blooded delivery. The former Eastern Daily Press reporter, now a best-selling international author and publisher, duly produced and presented his tuneful contribution to local culture.

He had promised as much to celebrate a return to reporting roots with a talk to Friends Of Norfolk Dialect at the Lophams Village Hall. The Diss area was his patch in the early 1960s.

An expectant gathering marvelled at the manner in which well-modulated vowels surrendered to a saucy feel for our vibrant vernacular. From Nat King Cole to The Singing Postman in one telling swoop.

Rapturous applause greeted the bold Grey rendition of Dwile, a song he claims to have rescued from an ancient, beer-stained music case, along with a mouldy, smelly floorcloth, in a piano stool in a pub near Stratton Strawless.

These highly original lyrics were sent repeatedly to Robbie Williams and many producers of West End Musicals for proposed inclusion in their repertoires. So far, said Mr Grey, no response has been traced from any of them.

If the musical establishment continues to snub the song, he may record it himself on the Fond label. "We reckon that could wholly wipe the floor with that Pop Idle lot" suggested a Fond spokesman.

While the jostling begins for a slice of exciting Norfolk action, judge for yourself the likely impact of these lines first aired on a Sunday afternoon at the Lophams Palladium:-

Middle Age is that awkward period when Father Time starts catching up on Mother Nature.

DWILE

Use a dwile
If you spill some hummus
With olive oil
Down yar Aunty's bloomers
As they dry by her fire,
That'll soon soothe her ire,

Or if you slop
Half a jar of piccalilli
Down the front o' yar trousers
And feel pertickullarly silly
You'll soon see yar neighbours
Start to smile
If you flash yar dwile....

So if any form of spillage badness
Drives you to the brink of madness
Be it tea, milk or beer
Or somethin' warse,
Never fear!

That the time,
You must keep on wipin'
Dwile! What's the use o' gripin'
Yar life will never be a trial
If you use yar dwile...

One day the "don't knows" will get in. Then what will we do?
Just when your cup of happiness is nearly full, someone always
jogs your elbow

20
Golden Era

They might think it's all over. But have I got news for you! After much soul-searching, I have decided to blow the whistle on bribery and corruption rife in Norfolk sport during the so-called "golden era" of the 1950s.

Yes, it could be a trifle late in some cases where blatant perpetrators have gone to that Far Pavilion in the Sky, but the current climate encouraging full and frank confession has convinced me that certain stains must be removed from yesterday's shorts and flannels.

My little black book of unsporting skulduggery is on its way to the ICC (Itteringham Centre for Correction) in the hope of prompting full amnesty for those providing full evidence of spurious tactics employed in many of our villages as a matter of course.

At present, I am stopping short of a "name-and-shame" policy for two reasons. First, I was involved, albeit inadvertently, in some of the more salacious incidents relating to local cricket around Coronation time in 1953. Second, I have to take on board the inescapable fact that so was everyone else.

It could be difficult to summon the remnants of an entire parish population of nearly 50 years ago to testify before the Norfolk Commission for Sporting Truth and Reconciliation. So spontaneous appearances and admissions will be fostered for the time being.

While most of the alleged incidents centre on soccer and cricket, especially in cup competitions where one decision could spell delight or disaster, it is clear other sporting arenas were subjected to unwarranted pressures. I must stress, however, that

What do you call an unemployed jester? Nobody's fool.

there is no evidence of any money changing hands.

Mild intimidation, mostly in the shape of two pints presented before the game to officials by the home side, and hatch-fixing, an insidious ploy worked in village pubs to deny visiting darts teams vital refreshment, emerge as main causes for complaint.

There are examples of bail-tampering to facilitate decision-making for an uncertain umpire on a windy day, and sandwich-spiking to force dangerous visiting batsmen out of the fray at significant stages of their reply after tea. (Female sabotage suspected here). Conker-baking, goalpost-loosening, pitch-soaking, net-snipping, stump-shaving, bootlace-joining and roller-meddling also feature on the infamy file.

Taking care not to aim an accusing digit directly at any specific person, let me offer a few pointers to the way scurrilous strata-gems were commonplace in all areas of recreation. Some of these escapades have been referred to the Crown Prosecution Service, named after a pub where they took place:

- Linesmen accepts brace of pheasants at half-time in Primary Cup-tie near Dereham in September, 1951. Home team, 7-0 down at the interval, recover to fly into next round 8-7.
- Referee declines touchline collection at half-time in Primary Cup-tie near Dereham in October, 1951. Home team, 8-0 behind at the interval, go on to lose 29-0.
- Local farmer wins pillow fight on greasy pole at village fete near Fakenham for seventh successive time in July, 1952. Inspection reveals only one side of pole is greasy.
- Local parson wins bowling for pig contest at church fete near Swaffham for eighth successive year in June, 1953. Verger says he will stand down after running event since 1945.
- District dominoes final at pub near Litcham abandoned when favourites complain of too many spots before their eyes. Doctored drinks blamed for disruption in March, 1954. Teetotal outsiders win title as final is replayed.

Why isn't phonetics spelt the way it sounds?

- District darts final at pub near Mileham abandoned as favourites complain of dizzy spells. Board fixed to rotate whenever a double is landed. Rank outsiders, team of do-it-yourself enthusiasts, take crown when final is replayed in March, 1955.
- Cricket umpire collects "player of year" award at annual dinner of village club near Longham in November, 1956. His son, captain and opening bowler, celebrates record 150 wickets in season, 137 of them lbw decisions.
- Verger wins bowling for pig contest at church fete near Swaffham for fourth successive year in June, 1957. Local parson says he enjoys running this event.

Winston the Singing Farmer – ploughing his own furrows around Norfolk and beyond.

Never lend people money. It gives them amnesia.

A BIT O' BINDERSTRING

I knew Bill Bates what used ter work fer Drake's at Badger's End
There wunt a tewl abowt the farm this fella couldn't mend
From a hayfork to a harvester, or any blessed thing
Ol' Bill could allus fix it with a bit o' binderstring.

One day the Fresian bull got out, and raged and tore around,
No-one dast go near 'im as he roared and pawed the ground
Til Boss shout; "Bill! the bull's got out and bin an' brook his ring!"
And Bill lassoed the buggar..... wi' a bit o' binderstring.

Bill courted Mabel for seven year, and then he say "Less wed
I got a table an' some chairs and Granny's feather bed.
There's half a ton o'tearters up in yonder field as I kin bring
And I med some handsome doormats out o' this here binderstring."

"Well" Mabel say "We'd best be wed afore they cut the hay"
So they had a slap-up wedding on the seventeenth of May.
But when they got ter chatch Bill found he'd gorn an' lorst the ring
So he hatter marry Mabel with a loop o' binderstring.

Next year a little mawther cum ter bless the happy pair
Wi' gret blue eyes like saucers and a tuft o' ginger hair
An' Bill he say ter parson at the little'uns christening
"See her hair is just the colour of a bit o' binderstring."

Well tyme go on an Ole Bill died and cum ter Heaven's door
He hear 'em all a'singing there and he wuz worried sore
He say ter good St Peter "Sar, I never larnt ter sing,
I was allus busy mendin' things wi' bits o' binderstring."

"Dunt worry, bor" St Peter say, "The Good Lord understands
He're bin a carpenter and like ter see folk use their hands
We're wholly glad ter see yer here, we've plenty who kin sing
But we need a handy chap like yew woss brought some binderstring."

So Bill he live in Heaven now. He's wholly happy there
He're got a little workshop just behind St Peter's chair
And while the angels play their harps and all them saints dew sing
Bill mend the little cherubs toys wi' bits o' binderstring.

Find an aim in life before you run out of ammunition.

21

Calling Cards

What do you call a collection of town criers? A poser design-ed to keep me guessing on the podium at Sheringham.

I was invited to crown the carnival queen and meet her atten-dants. Our colourful guard of honour certainly raised the decibel level of this happy occasion.

It had to be voted missionary work of the highest order for a lad from Cromer, although I had been assured Crab Wars hostili-ties would be put to one side while Shannocks and their friends celebrated.

Just to make sure I came to no harm, a quavering quartet in their quintessentially eye-catching uniforms kept me company along crowded streets.

Tony Nelson (Sheringham), David Bullock (Norwich), Kerry Hart (Swaffham) and Jason Bell (Cromer) exchanged the sort of banter you'd expect from extrovert characters mixing local pride with a common cause.

Home advantage scarcely clouded Mr Nelson's horizons, even though he may have put undue emphasis on the "old" when intro-ducing his much-valued old friend who shouts the odds and shakes the bell for Cromer.

I was urged to tease the large gathering with that question about a group of town criers. "What do you call this lot?" drew some surprisingly polite responses.

"A peal" called a woman almost smothered by children and bal-loons. "The Clangers" suggested a hairy-chested man dipping into his television memory bank. "Belladonnas - just like prima donnas, only noisier!" chortled a bright boy, who admitted he was only there to see the carnival queen.

Humour is like a frog. If you dissect it, then it dies.

A peal of bellringers on parade at Sheringham Carnival

A little girl called Tracey from Melton Constable came up with the correct answer. "A bellow" she whispered, and collected her prize from Mr Bullock, who has looked into such matters at a top level collective for town criers.

With my crowning duties done in the sun, I ambled back to the Lobster pub, our carnival day headquarters, for a pint and a pun or two. My companions teetered on the bellicose as one bad line followed another.

These were the best, from four fine fellows who dress up at the drop of a hat to make important announcements:

- What did the town crier call his memoirs? After The Bawl Was Over.
- A town crier who liked rhythm and blues music was known as the Shriek of R'n'B.
- Where do naughty female town criers finish up? Hollerway Prison.
- Then there was the town crier who gave up because he was ashamed of his calling ...

If a thing goes without saying - let it.

I meet The Clodhoppers on a Suffolk safari. Ray Edwards and
Graham Cole make colourful company.

Just the ticket! Press Gang passengers line up for the last train to Squitville.

Poverty is hereditary. You get it from your children.

22

Local Olympics

Exciting news of a Norfolk bid to stage the Olympic Games in 2052, albeit lodged in the fervent hope of being allowed to include a few home-grown pursuits.

Main events would go ahead in the Colkirk Coliseum, due to be built with lottery backing and a grant from the Manchester United players' benevolent fund, while communities all over the county prepare for their own sporting showdown.

Wrestling at Flordon, show jumping at Walcott, hairdressing at Crimplesham and troshing at Swaffham have already attracted keen support from the IOC (Itteringham Obstacle Course) organisers.

The following await official registration before the final choice for medal missions is made just after the World Cup semi-finals at Barton Turf.

- Rock climbing at Alpington
- Rodeo riding at Old Buckenham
- Chicken plucking at Great Moulton
- Jelly making at Hethersett
- Flint collecting at Knapton
- Bell ringing at Pulham St Mary
- Rowing at Sculthorpe
- Reed cutting at Sedgeford
- Apple bobbing at Syderstone
- Hedge trimming at Thornage
- Road sweeping at Broome
- Strawberry gathering at Pickenham
- Eating contest at Burston

Everybody is ignorant, only on different subjects.

- Carpentry at Shelfanger
- Lamp lighting at Hardwick
- Locksmithing at Stiffkey
- Knife sharpening at Honing
- Police wrestling at Melton Constable
- Straw collecting at Bale
- 1500 metres at Mileham
- Lumberjack contest at Lopham
- Banger racing at Carbrooke
- Fisticuffs at Clenchwarton
- Bungee jumping at Attlebridge
- Dubious results at Diddlington
- Marathon at Runhall
- Tossing the caber at Wood Rising
- Bull-fighting at Horningtoft
- Very Long Distance Walk at Limpenhoe
- Underground Pole Vaulting at Norton Subcourse

Fringe events include: sponsored mardling at Gasthorpe, finding fault with everything at Tuttington and being content with bronze at Winfarthing.
Over to you, Mr Starter!

Where it all started in 1984 – and ended in 2008. I doff my hat to the wonderful theatre on Cromer Pier.

Writer's block - numb de plume.

Hero worship. Lifeboat legend Henry Blogg is always worth a
visit on Cromer seafront.

The end does not always justify the jeans.

23

Rumlot O' Squit

An invitation to take liberal liberties with our vibrant vernacular produced a veritable vaudeville of entertaining entries. In short, a rare scalder o' squit!

I challenged readers of my column in the Eastern Daily Press to come up with original collective nouns with that distinctive Norfolk flavour to match groups of people or objects familiar on the local scene. Some, inevitably, were less than flattering about the likes of estate agents, second-homers and caravaners – while mobile phones, I was delighted to report, were roundly ridiculed.

Most, inspiringly, were packed with genuine Norfolk passion, power and purpose in the name of a dialect gloriously suitable for such an exercise. Perhaps a few will be freely adopted in years to come as hard-pressed natives continue to feel threatened by the march of so-called progress.

Main salute to Tony Bradstreet of Attleborough. He sent me a long list of collective nouns for each subject, so I whittled it down to my 10 favourites:

- A smarmhiggle of estate agents
- A furrerbred of tractor drivers
- A peripapightle of second-homers
- A hallereen of mobile phones
- A marshterpiece of bird watchers
- A dodmankew of caravaners
- A beachcromer of crab fishermen
- A troshellhop of first-time buyers
- A searleground of wind turbines
- A baleful of combine harvesters

These are the good old days. Just you wait and see.

Runners-up prizes went to Judy Gowing of Mattishall and Lorna Lincoln of Spalding.

Judy's selection included a mudruckerin' of tractor drivers, a lugstuckle of mobile phones, a bunkshifty of caravaners and a cornquafferin' of combine harvesters.

Lorna excelled by calling estate agents houseummevers and followed with twitchlurking of bird watchers and a confuzzling of combine harvesters.

Trish Thorpe of Rocklands unveiled a fluence of estate agents, a voidem of caravaners and a porlot of first-time buyers.

Ann English of Whissonsett went for a lugdinging of mobile phones, a borrowing of first-time buyers and a pinch of crab fishermen.

Mick Barber of North Walsham pointed to a qupbehinder of tractor drivers and described bird watchers as harnserhunters and crab fishermen as sidewalkers.

TORK PROPER

A rash of groovy labels on everyday items continues to dominate our language. But salvation is nigh.

Trendybabble must make way for propaspeak, sensible, old-fashioned Norfolk words and expressions. Try these for size, my ole bewties, and then come up with your own alternatives.

- Worse-case scenario – suffin bad
- Positive feedback – wholly good
- At the end of the day – shuttin-up time
- Level playing field – hent bin built on – yit.
- At this moment in time – 'bowt now, I reckun
- Can you run that past me again? – sorry, wunt listenin'
- Hear what you say – dunt tork ser sorft!
- I see where you're coming from – ye dunt fewl me!
- When all is said and done – thass yer lot!
- Let's run this up the flagpole and see who salutes – hent got a clue woss gorn on!

People in a temper often say a lot of silly things they really mean.

So that's where all the old material comes from! On stage at the Pavilion Theatre in Cromer with a handy wheelie-bin.

Do crabs think we walk sideways?

24

Scary Squit

A Halloween production at Sheringham's Little Theatre in harness with local historian and author Neil Storey provided the perfect excuse to mix squit with serious culture.

I had to dig deep to come up with suitably creepy yarns for the occasion, but a selection of North Norfolk ghost stories that may have been largely forgotten sent a shudder through a full house.

Spooks, Squeal 'n' Squit brought a fresh dimension to local history. I don't think Neil, for all his scholarly expertise, had even heard of some of these...

- The Wobbly Witch of Weybourne, who rides a sit-up-and-beg bicycle on the beach when there's a full moon and sings shanties before she disappears. It is rumoured she turned into a lay-by in 1567.

- The Bewtiful Banshee of Bodham, believed to be the reincarnation of a 17th century commuter who moans inconsolably if Sanders' bus fails to stop in the village on February 30th. She has bought a season ticket for the entire coastal run.

- The Lost Sherpa of Sheringham, whose cries are heard on stormy nights in November as he tries to scale the notorious north face of Beeston Bump without the aid of a safety net.

Spooky fun with local historian Neil Storey.

Always use tasteful words. You may have to eat them.

- The Mad Monk of Morston, who tries to get rid of some of his dirty habits on the marshes "before yon blackberrye harveste be complet." He draws big crowds in September with his unusual dance featuring an invisible dog... Up The Creek Without a Poodle.

- The Seven Samphire Sisters of Salthouse make regular midnight appearances in the roadside garden of the Dun Cow public house towards he end of the tourist season. The length of their dresses, usually taffeta, give an indication as to what sort of season it has been... longer the dress, better the results.

- The Khaki King of Kelling, a first world war soldier who leads a one-man charge across the heath when no-one is looking on any fine night in April. He is repelling all invaders down below who have arrived without passports after disembarking from "that old German Ocean."

- The Crazy Croupier of Cromer, a dashing figure in dinner suit with red carnation buttonhole and waxed moustache. He haunts the beach at West Runton on alternate Mondays in June looking for a pair of aces to complete a winning hand at the Beeston Regis Casino-de-luxe... Tradition has it he lost all his chips to a girl called Mary-Jane.

- The Blasted Blighter of Blakeney – is the ghost of an old salt who haunts Blakeney Harbour at Regatta time and shouts "Rollocks!" at anyone wearing green wellies and "avast behind" at any female celebrity he can spot.

- The Malevolent Madam of Mundesley – this is the ghost of Greta who kept a notorious house of ill-repute in the 1800s down Legover Lane near Come-and-get-me Alley. Some high class clients from Trimingham and Walcott are alleged to have done away with her after she threatened to tell all – for a small

It's easier to put on slippers than carpet the whole world.

fee – to the North Norfolk News. But she had her revenge when their houses fell into the sea on a winter's night in 1872.

- The Clairvoyant Clergyman of Cley – this is the spirit of a 16th century parson in the village who forecast it would become rather posh as soon as all the locals had been found council houses. The Rev Septimus Mount was defrocked and sent to Stiffkey after scandalising the Cley congregation with his sermon entitled "I'm a Celibate, Get me Out of Here!"

- The Love-Lorn Lass of Langham – her wraith and her wails of anguish can be seen and heard at the back of the old Doctor's Surgery in this desirable village. Yes, she was turned down on medical grounds by her sailor-boy lover home from the sea. He found another in Wells. He found another in Binham. And he found another in Gunthorpe. He finished up with a debutante from Beeston Regis. They had 17 children – and so lived nappily ever after ...

Music and mirth combined...Ian Prettyman, Pat Maitland and Colin Burleigh.

Spot the odd one out... Pat Nearney with Gal Liza and Mawther Sheilah.

Diet - a plan for putting off tomorrow what you put on today.

25
Sparring Partners

If I had a pound for every time I heard someone say "If I had a pound for every time...." – well, we'd both be rich.

We echo each other constantly, but there's merit to come back if we do it to show gratitude at finding someone else sparky enough to put the world to rights with a no-nonsense nugget minted before it got dark over Will's mother's.

Television and other branches of "popular culture" may have blurred too many simple lines of communication – y'know what I mean you guys like at this moment in time – but there remains a defiant and colourful rump sticking it out against crass uniformity.

I've been on the prowl along the edge of linguistic daring, ready to bless those clinging to rocks of individuality in a boiling sea of sameness. It brings such joy to an old Norfolk heart when homely voices rise above the turgid tumult.

A cheery exchange in the middle of Cromer the other morning between two lively indigenous remnants, one several years older than his sparring partner, told me we were ready to face the summer invasion with customary wit, repartee and a reasonable measure of tolerance.

Flotsam and Jetski (made-up names to protect the guilty) wasted no time on polite formalities as a small crowd gathered on the pavement eager for instant entertainment. Here are edited highlights, phonetically modified to help those unfamiliar with the Norfolk tongue:

Flotsam: "Cor, blarst, is that really you lookin' so well?"
Jetski: "Thass me. They told me you wuz dead..."

Ego -something which enables people to live with themselves.

Flotsam: "No, only the good die young and leave the bad to better tharselves."

Jetski: "Wuh, half the lies you tell ent true – and I ent sure about the other half either."

Flotsam: "Thass bloomin' sight better than torkin' in yards an' thinkin' in inches."

Jetski: "Git yar brain out o' neutral, ole partner, an' lend us a fiver so I can do missionary work in Sherin'am."

Flotsam: "Can't afford it, but I'll give you 50p as insensitive to go abroad."

Jetski: "You're so tight you wunt give anyone a fright if you wuz a ghost..."

So it breezed on, a double act worthy of top billing at the end of the pier. I don't know how much was rehearsed or a repeat of previous fond encounters, but it made a delightful change from mobile phone babble or predictable grouses about the weather, last night's television and the price of strawberries.

The hand of friendship extended with one admonishing finger at the ready is at the heart of Norfolk

Former Cromer lifeboat coxswain Richard Davies shows his skill at traditional step-dancing.

He who laughs, lasts.

drollery and can still serve as a useful weapon in Homewatch circles. Strangers with nothing to hide should accept a forceful "Hent sin yew around these parts afore" as a good-natured inquiry asking for a chat.

While dialect, native cunning and laughter form a potent force in the battle to salvage something of our precious local identity there's always scope for a small pebble of gentle reflection to be dropped in the well of Norfolk life. I caught a few ripples recently in a seafront mardle with an old fisherman.

He had been invited to a barbecue that evening and chuckled gently as he made comparisons: "They used to feed inside and go down the garden to the privy. Now they have the privy inside and feed in the garden." Crackling edge of social history.

We had a neighbour in Hevingham who polished up a single joke for use whenever he saw me dallying in the garden. I soon learned to play dumb...

"How do you find a woman out?"

"I don't know, George, how do you find a woman out?"

"Easy, you go round when she ent there."

Uncanny echoes of my role as a simple foil some 40 years earlier along the dusty lane of childhood in my home village of Beeston. I asked the local sage where he was going. "I ent a'goin' nowhere, boy" he twinkled. "I'm just a'comin' back."

That was long before our lives became digital and dynamic, before getting from one place to another became simply a matter of speed rather than a chance to enjoy a friendly chat. Of course, far more folk strolled and biked and the general pace simply encouraged amiable encounters all the way.

Well, high summer in Cromer town centre, with traffic at a standstill and pavements clogged, can inspire a revivalist spirit. And it really doesn't matter then if we do talk in yards and think in inches.

If the man who invented the drawing board had got it wrong, what would he have gone back to?

26

Grey Power

The good, the bad and the seemingly inevitable all vie for attention as North Norfolk prepares to welcome charabancs packed with discerning tourists.

"Crusty old Cromer", starring multi-coloured commodes on the clifftop and deck chairs with panic buttons below, seems better equipped than most to cater for the more mature trippers. "Shady old Sheringham", offering half-price hair cuts and help with holiday heating, and "Moody old Mundesley", where nude sunbathing nearly comes up to your expectations, are beginning to make inroads into the lucrative grey market. But Cromer easily leads the way.

It's all to do with embracing change – reinventing, rebranding, regenerating, revamping, reviving, reanimating, refurbishing and reverberating with bold ideas. Take the Norwich Road entrance into town as the parish church and sea paint a gloriously welcoming picture. Where else can you find such a stirring example of a Murray Walker-inspired design coupled with genuine feeling for a foreign tongue?

When the new junior school went up at the side of that alarmingly busy thoroughfare, drivers were encouraged to slow down and to learn how to pronounce "chicane". Half of them still don't know what it's for but they appreciate it is a different sort of challenge and aesthetically superior to Gorleston's Cresta Run.

That sort of vision can only hasten the return of mixed bathing machines and a regular change of accumulator to keep the wireless system going in boarding houses and the lifeboat shed.

In my capacity as unofficial tourism advisor to the district council, an unpaid post with no discernable perks apart from a

Golf scores are directly proportional to the number of witnesses.

free bus pass to Sidestrand – you walk back – I have prepared a discussion document entitled: "Putting New Punch Into Poppyland – Make It Scott-Free". Main thrust is to drain away all those flowery Victorian images of genteel picnics and poetry readings in the Garden of Sleep and replace them with a dynamic website aimed at trendy and affluent pensioners with a clean mobility scooter driving licence.

Stand by for www.elasticstocking.com boasting the only genuine Blogg in the world. It must open up countless fresh channels of pleasure to growing flocks of over-80s heading for the fleshpots of Cromer and District. That tired old label "Sagalouts" has to be unpeeled in favour of positive images like "Epiloggers" and "Timecheaters" as the wrinkly revolution hits the Costa del Crabland.

Outline planning permission has been granted for a nifty old folks' nightclub near the hospital. Dentchers – "No entry after Emmerdale" – will advise patrons to remove teeth before crowd surfing or samphire suppers. Lifts back to sheltered accommodation courtesy of a friendly milkman may be allowed following Friday extensions featuring old party favourites such as You've Been Zimmerframed and Sedation, Sedation, Sedation.

Talking of banality television, I also bring important news from the real world, based as usual in North Norfolk.

A retirement home with a big difference will go up soon as close to the brink as possible at Happisburgh. It will cater exclusively for folk who want to pull out of the rat-race they were never invited to join in the first place.

Inquiries are mounting for rooms at "Dunnoffin" – or "Llareggub" for Welsh speakers – after a national campaign bearing the legend: "I'm A Non-Entity, Get Me Into There!" In direct contrast to dear old Burnham Market and other stylish pockets where genuine celebrities and their companions add lustre to Norfolk's growing reputation as the place to be – if only at weekends – the

An exaggeration is only a truth that lost its temper.

Boats take a well-deserved rest on Cromer beach.

Happisburgh refuge will house just hopeless cases washed up on the shore of utter disregard.

"A facility such as this is long overdue" said former Trumpton and Hector's House choreographer and prompt Orville Dack, who will run the home with his partner, ex-*Top of the Pops* wardrobe mistress and Sunday Trumpet agony aunt, Daisy Cutter.

The Happisburgh clifftop location has been selected deliberately to deter intrusion into private grief. "These poor souls simply want to accept quickly and quietly what they never were, and you just can't do that with silly autograph hunters and prying cameras all over the place" added Daisy.

North Norfolk District Council has raised no objections to plans for the project although it has made it abundantly clear that should the building topple onto the beach below but still remain largely intact, it may count it as a second home eligible for double council tax.

Orville and Daisy are looking for someone completely unknown, unbecoming and unimportant to open their retreat, "Perhaps we'll select from the first inmates" they smiled.

"Or just do it ourselves."

There are no new sins. The old ones just get more publicity.

RUM OLE NEARMES

Moost counties hev nearmes searm'as Norfolk
Whot never sound quite loike they spell.
So, because I'm a trew Norfolk dumplin'
I fare ter know some onnem well.

Now, why should Wy-mond-ham be Windham?
And Happ-is-burgh's Haisboro, yew see,
And Haut-bois ..... well, thass known as Hobbies.
They reckun thass French - dunt arsk me!

There's By-laugh whot lay close ter Dereham,
Called Belaw, at least so they say,
And Gar-bold-is-ham - well, jist leave out the middle
Then Garblesham's the trew Norfolk way.

There's Colney, well, thass known as Coney,
An' Cost-ess-ey thass Cossey fer sure.
Hindol-vest-on is well known as Hilderstun,
But please dunt arsk me what for!

The old folk at Wive-ton say Wiffen,
An' the neartives of Cley will say Clay,
While Glandford's referred to as Glanfer,
Thass torkin' the trew Norfolk way.

The Norfolk for Salt-house is Saltus,
An' Morston - just leave out the T.
While Stody is allus called Study,
That dew seem a rum'un ter me.

There's Stiffkey what locals call Stukey
An' their cockles are called Stukey Blews.
Thow, o'course, the village med headlines
When the parson wuz well in the news.

This list ent complete I assure yew,
But these few are a proof jist ter show
Thass right trew whot the rhyme say o' Norfolk ....
"We allus dew diffrunt, yer know!"

A closed mouth gathers no feet.

27

Misery Month

August is the cruellest month, especially for cricket-lovers when football, Olympic Games and carnival capers steal all the headlines and attract additional downpours.

Pubs aren't what they used to be, particularly if you want to make half of bitter and a whole pickled egg last the best part of some time up the corner.

So it's good to discover one establishment not far from the enticing North Norfolk coast where passing fads and fancies receive short shrift. The Dewdrop Inn at Lower Dodman is slowly establishing itself as the county's least trendy pub. "We are at the blunt end of social awareness and celebrity culture" boasts landlord Jason Bullard.

He invites regulars to raise a tankard in honour of Fuller Pilch every night before pumps are drawn. "FP is better than KP" is the latest toast. A portrait of the Norfolk master batsman of Victorian times takes guard over the bar. Young Bill Edrich cover drives in the snug.

Football banter is banned until Norwich City reach the last 16 of any cup competition. Comments on the Olympics are confined to "circumcised swimming", Sue Barker's idea of colour co-ordination and the number of rings under the eyes of pub customers guilty of watching all night. A full set earns a packet of porky scratchings and a jumper knitting pattern.

Dewdrop Inn regulars respond with vigour and invention to all government initiatives to tackle anti-social behaviour. A pledge to cut after-hours drinking by at least 25% is by 2020 is going well although retired coypu catcher Ernie Hoskins and retired stack thatcher Horry Barnes both abstained when it came to the vote.

Gardening tip - best time to take cuttings is when no-one is looking.

They accepted in principle the idea of licensees being allowed some sleep before reopening.

Main plank in this hostelry's "rustic revival" platform, however, concerns abolition of the happy hour. It is in the process of being replaced by the misery month.

"With parliament in recess and most other top thinkers on holiday, we saw a real opening to set a good example to the rest of the country" enthused landlord Bullard. "In any case, our happy hour has been anything but for at least two decades, with customers moaning and groaning about everything from the price of salted peanuts to the over-hasty disbandment of Lower Dodman Home Guard."

Retired muckspreader Billy Archer, a fully paid-up member of the scattering classes, admitted he had used the happy hour exclusively to blast the brewery and anyone else responsible for the spiralling cost of his mild beer. "It's wholly ridiculous... I'm always pleased when I've had enough of it."

The great Dewdrop Inn experiment started on August 1 with every customer urged to bring grumbles great and small to the counter. "Our melancholy manifesto must ensure safer streets, homes, allotments, farmyards, bus shelters and bowling greens because the pub is the only place where complaining aloud is allowed" said Ernie Hoskins.

"I just hope I can get through a full month without cracking. It's simply a matter of curbing my natural instincts to smile, sing and look on the bright side and pick an argument wherever I can instead" added Horry Barnes.

Retired socialite Felicity Rockland-Ffynche, newcomer to the parish after a glittering career as leader of the chattering classes in Norwich's Golden Triangle, warned against a misery month for starters. She preferred a woebegone week or forbidding fortnight but eventually bowed to majority wishes. Retired stenographer Cicely Bartrum, darts club social secretary, considered it right to

If all the world's a stage, where's the audience sitting?

cancel this year's mystery outing to Mundesley, not only to prevent the bus driver from winning the usual competition to guess their destination but also to "put down a marker in our campaign to curb over-heated behaviour."

Semi-retired dishwasher Elsie Wedgewood has entered strongly into the proper spirit by placing a new notice over the Sinkers & Swimmers Restaurant doorway. It reads: "Whine and dine – and then have a good beef at the bar."

Her part-time assistant, former laundry worker Nellie Droy, has also been busy in the nappy-changing room behind the dining area, pinning up news that "gripe water will be provided if you whimper long enough."

Mine host Bullard, clearly anticipating the interest of television crews and tabloid imbibers during August's silly season, is confident his rural free house can liberate an exciting national movement.

"We call it whinge drinking. Mix that with a grouse-more image and typical Norfolk belligerence – and the misery month could go top of the social calendar.

I salute the Waveney Wonders, David Woodward and Brian Patrick

The Youth Policy in action... Greg Powles and Robin Skipper tease Danny Platton

A bore is a man with a glass in one hand and your lapel in the other.

I think we turn left at Blo Norton if the wind is in the east. A good map reader is essential on these strange rural rounds

Old gardeners never die. They just spade away.

28
Jam Session

My wife was lost behind a cloud of fruity vapour rising like a sudden fog from her kitchen cauldron.

I resisted a strong temptation to chant:

When shall we two eat again?
In thunder, lightning or in rain?

She would only have replied pointedly:

You'll get your dinner after one,
When the strawberry jam is done.

How on earth did Rupert and his Nutwood chums think of all those rhyming couplets so quickly? Is that the most durable trait of anthropomorphic characters? Did Mrs Bear make her boy's check trousers out of material left over from a parachute?

That fruity vapour was getting to me as I played my customary key role in home-made jam production... staying well clear of boiling and stirring operations until a professional taster was needed. I tried another tack after devouring the newspaper from cover to cover.

"Did you know, I'm slightly older than Sooty but a bit younger than Joan Collins?" I'd moved almost imperceptivity from one childhood favourite to another. Then dear Sooty came into the equation.

Now, didn't Harry Corbett have a hand in his rise to stardom? (Not to be confused with Steptoe Junior, who carried an extra H on his cart) Yes, I saw them working together in Yarmouth in the mid-1960s at a special children's event in Deneside Methodist Church, if I recall correctly. Sooty may have gone more ecumen-

Nothing makes a person more productive than the last minute.

ical after a rousing rendition of that grand old hymn, Gladly My Cross-Eyed Bear.

I was there in my capacity as punning correspondent for the Yarmouth Mercury. Mike Farman, my showbiz colleague from the Eastern Daily Press, was a bit embarrassed when Uncle Harry invited us all to wave to his little friend in the pulpit. Mike said he felt silly saluting a puppet. I told him not to be such a grumpy old spoil-sport.

No rhyming couplets for Sooty. Just squirts, nifty nods, the odd neck-crunching swivel and a sharp clip round the lug with his lethal wand. An ideal community policeman of the old school. "Izzy Wizzy, let's get busy cutting crime figures."

Official tasting services not yet required. More simmering and stirring first. I mused on.

"Wasn't there a pop group called The Jam? And what about dear old Marmalade? Gladys Knight and the Pips?" Now I was on a pop and rock nostalgia roll although I couldn't convince myself there had been a close-harmony group in the 1930s called Bottled Fruit.

From nowhere I plucked Cherry Ripe, Blueberry Hill, Strawberry Fields For Ever, Sugar and Spice, Banana Boat Song and anything by Buffet Sainte Marie. You can cheat a bit as vapours rise.

Who else would I want round that steaming cauldron to add genuine flavour to home-made products? Cream, Sweet, Crystals, Honeycombs, Lovin' Spoonful, Chuck Berry and Eden Kane for starters. Mustn't ignore Canned Heat. And we ought to find a spot for Nancy Whiskey, Lena Martell and Little Ginny.

"Make us a cup of tea" suggested the wife as she turned down the heat and turned on the charm. I was almost lured into the Earl Grey Whistle Test trap...but I knew that could lead so easily to the Beverage Sisters, Saucerer's Apprentice and Slow Boat to China.

Smokers are people who puff on cigars, cigarettes and steps.

I suppose psychiatrists would call it a useful journey in word association, employing tenuous links to jump from one field to another without catching your credibility on the electric fencing.

I blame grammar school education in Norfolk during the late 1950s, especially those teachers who smiled admiringly when the very mention of Copernicus prompted cries of "Dig the underwear!"

One mentor actively encouraged an early form of lateral thinking, asking us to imagine what certain characters from history and fiction might say to each other if fate threw them together.

I soon had Sir Robert Walpole, with a proud Norfolk accent, asking young David Copperfield if he knew why Barkis wuz willin' and when Yarmouth would merge with Lowestoft. Then along came Horatio Nelson to see if Peggotty could get away for a quiet night out in the Burnhams.

"Slightly parochial, Skipper, but shows promise." Story of my life. Like being kept in for telling slightly risqué stories at the back of the classroom. One strawberry said to another: "If we hadn't been in that bed together, we wouldn't be in this jam right now...."

"You can have a taste now" came a voice from the kitchen. I went, I licked, I concurred with a "perfect" verdict.

Roll on the blackberry season!

Three Parts Light... I team up with singer Danny Platton and comedian Pat Nearney for another night out.

The trouble with true humility is that you can't talk about it.

Must be a really posh dew!

Ian Prettyman, another Press Gang
stalwart, on melodeon

Even I can keep pace with these!
Making friends outside the black-
smith's forge at Heydon

Festival fun – on stage with
Mundesley favourite Phil Drackett
in the Coronation Hall, a double act
which lasted for several years

Sign in window of closed-down bookshop - "Words failed us".

29

Sands of Time

There's a useful myth, possibly fed and watered by tourism touts, that seashore regulars are cosy, caring and sensitive souls. From bronzed young lifeguards full of morning freshness to rheumy-eyed old salts twinkling in their evening sun, our golden sands play host to the sort of close-knit community we used to find everywhere.

Sorry, but this charming survivor of the good old days is but an invention of over-heated imaginations, over-blown holiday brochures and a desperate clinging to the wreckage of Ealing Comedy capers, Hi-di-Hi campers and Five Go Up to Bikini Top.

That's my honest verdict after countless safaris in all seasons and in all weathers on and around Cromer beach. Last time I got really excited? A Sunday in November, 1993 when the pier was sliced in two by a runaway barge in howling wind and lashing rain.

Don't read me wrong. I didn't rejoice in such dramatic damage to one of my favourite fresh-air suppliers, but it felt good to have a bit more animated company than usual as darkness fell.

It's been fairly quiet since although they did knock down the delightful old Rocket House Cafe at the bottom of The Gangway to make room for a lifeboat museum with restaurant above. That's progress... but old Blogg and his sou-westered diners still go down to the galley for wittles and yarns.

I squeeze through a huddle of tractors and boats and echoes to find the water's edge. Fishermen are usually too busy sorting out hauls to drop anchor for a mardle. Solo strollers, counting foot-prints behind them without looking, clearly need their solitude. Occasionally a woman of indeterminate years and wearing

The best way to save face is to keep the lower half shut.

sensible shoes will scan the skies, twirl her parasol and offer a free forecast, but most wanderers keep their powder dry.

Early summer trippers, a sort of advance party sent in to test the going, skulk behind multi-coloured windbreaks to avoid any passing local eccentric barmy enough to ask where they come from. Beach hut owners gently open the door on a new dawning. Dog owners wonder if they ought to check dates for allowing Black Shuck to rampage unchecked across certain stretches of sand.

There's no disguising a lack of adventure. My spies tell me it's about the same all along our coast. I'll check for myself, armed with a few handy examples of how Norfolk seaside life really was a beach for Victorian trailblazers.

My copy of The Cromer and North Walsham Post for August 23, 1890, arrived a few weeks ago to spotlight proper fun and games

A favourite walk along the clifftop path at Cromer, looking back at town and pier.

A born loser is someone who takes a girl to the Tunnel of Love - and she tells him to wait outside

on the sands where I yearn for a little modern action. An editorial thundered: "We have been urged both by visitors and residents to raise a protest against the bathing of men and women within the same area.

"Those degraded creatures who have no sense of propriety in this respect will have to seek a beach unfrequented by persons worthy of being described as ladies and gentlemen.

"Sometimes whole families will enter a bathing machine, regardless of the fact that it is in the midst of the ladies' ground, and there both sexes will go through their natatory exercises to the disgust of those who have hired the surrounding machines."

Degradation indeed. Reckon this has the makings of a gripping new television reality show – Call My Buff, Navel Revue or I'm a Mixed Bather, Get Me Into There! spring to mind – and just think what that could do for Cromer's "living in the past" reputation.

Annie Berlyn, compiling her book Sunrise-Land, Rambles in Eastern England, in 1894, painted this enticing picture of Yarmouth beach as a "scene of wild orgies on the part of excited excursionists." Want to know more?

"They come to 'enjoy' themselves, and for that purpose they hie them to the shining sands, wherein they dig holes and deposit their many babies, duly provided with feeding bottles, while they themselves, fortified at the frequent and conveniently adjacent saloons, dance to the strains of piano-organs, cornets and various other musical instruments."

Yes, a pop festival with progressive child-care provision. And remember this is a resort which flagged up an all-purpose solution to the vexed questions of affordable housing, renewable energy and coastal erosion – an old boat on the beach with an iron funnel sticking out of it for a chimney.

Peggotty's abode. Mixed bathing machines. Bunkered babies. Telling carbon-free imprints on the sands of time.

The only thing that grows thicker as you spread it is rumour.

Barbershop singers file in as I compere a concert in Norwich

More culinary capers in the Radio Norfolk kitchen.

Modesty is the gentle art of enhancing your charm by pretending not to be aware of it.

30

Crowning Touch

A letter from 10, Downing Street in London could mean only one thing – Tony Blair wanted some new lines laced with squit to take to Prime Minister's Question Time. In fact, it was much more important than that. But I had to keep a secret for just over six weeks.

My appointment as a Member of the Order of the British Empire (MBE) was duly announced in the Queen's New Year Honours List for 2007. A wonderful award only four years after becoming a Deputy Lieutenant of Norfolk and the crowning touch in my career as writer, broadcaster and entertainer.

It takes something unusual to lure me out of Norfolk. It takes something extraordinary to take me into the capital. I felt obliged to wash thoroughly behind my ears and dress up properly for a family outing to Buckingham Palace. Here's my diary account for Wednesday, March 21, 2007:

The big day dawns cold but bright. I dress up in my Moss Bros gear, feeling rather overdone as the taxi takes us to the Palace. We receive crystal clear instructions from a team of experts who ensure big events like this run smoothly. I'm among the last to be called into the Grand Ballroom to meet the Queen and receive my MBE.

She refers to my journalism with the Eastern Daily Press and my writing in the vernacular. She admits she finds it rather difficult to read. I tell her I tend to write it very slowly so it's not too hard to understand. She smiles approvingly. Time only for a brief mardle before the royal handshake, orderly retreat, boxing up of the medal and joining the throng.

Nothing dispels enthusiasm like a small admission fee.

Then it's on to the scrimmage in the courtyard where photographers are waiting. Danny locates the girl camera operator from the Press Association who is taking a special shot of me, top hat, medal and all, for the Eastern Daily Press.

I rejoin Diane, Danny and Robin for family pictures and call the reporters' office in Cromer to pass on a few immediate reflections for tomorrow's paper. Although it seems like an eternity waiting to be ushered into the royal presence, this tingling event is over all too soon.

Back to the hotel to change. Danny spearheads a quick look at some of London's delights as we take to the Underground. Hyde Park Corner, Covent Garden and Piccadilly Circus the main attractions as darkness falls.

I try to soak it all up, a lad from a Norfolk village in the big city to be honoured by the Queen. Here I am accompanied by my family who mean so much. They represent the larger Norfolk family who have nurtured me to this proud stage of a long Norfolk career in the public eye.

I relish my day in the spotlight – even if the capital excesses still leave me rather cold. Today is about human factors... although Gordon Brown's 11th budget is bound to steal some of the headlines from me.

England footballer Steve Gerrard and actress Penelope Keith were on parade at the same time for this investiture ceremony. I told Steve not to stray offside. I reminded Penelope that I had interviewed her on BBC Radio Norfolk's Dinnertime Show a few years earlier when she was appearing at Norwich Theatre Royal. Out of such moments are special memories moulded and stored away.

The local press made much of my short but meaningful exchange with the Queen. "Cor blarst me, thass right nice on'yer, m'ole bewty" ran the Eastern Daily Press headline, and there

Does anyone gossip about other people's secret virtues?

Skipper family proudly on parade at Buckingham Palace.

were various references to "King of Squit", a title I felt truly honoured to carry into such exalted circles. Some suggested MBE could stand for "Master of Bucolic Entertainment" although I preferred "My Bewtiful Embellishment".

My award for services to the Norfolk community surely had its roots in countless village halls where our precious humour and dialect found fresh impetus and joy with Press Gang concerts and many other truly local celebrations. Shaking buckets for charities and raising vital funds for local facilities simply added spice to the sort of exercise that used to be an automatic slice of community life.

Middle age - when the past was perfect and the present is tense.

I enthused many times to colleagues on stage as the squit revivalist spirit flowed: "Oh, how I wish we could bottle this and take it to parts in sore need of such refreshment!" The fact we often had as many newcomers to Norfolk in the audience as hardened natives clearly underlined the value of such missions, most notably in rural parts. We urged a new brand of togetherness to show itself.

Without labouring the issue, I did point up the irony of a proud parochialism earning me a national honour a decade or so after being shown the door by the BBC for bemoaning a sad loss of localness in much of Radio Norfolk's output. For the record, I did receive calls of congratulation from old colleagues on the station when news of my MBE was released.

The end of my full-time broadcasting career in 1995 did offer the incentive – as well as the need – to tackle a wider range of activities. Press Gang bookings multiplied along with other entertainment calls and there was also time to help set up Friends Of Norfolk Dialect to promote and preserve the local tongue in the face of so many Mummerzet abominations on television and radio. I was FOND's founder chairman for three years and then social secretary. I wrote more books (all about Norfolk) and worked on a series of DVDs and CDs featuring local people and places.

While the production line flourished, my family and true friends continued to line up confidently behind. There were all there when I savoured my little bit of Norfolk squit with my monarch at Buckingham Palace.

ESCAPE PLAN

Small boy to his father during an over-long sermon in a Norfolk church: "Daddy, if we give him the money now, do you reckon he'll let us go home?"

Sticker seen on car going through Cromer –
"If you can read this, I've lost my caravan."

Jazz enthusiasts Eric Clarke, Colin Burleigh and Mike Parle
tune up with me for a special musical broadcast

No wonder I put on weight with all this delicious food for thought.

**Parents often talk about the younger generation as if they didn't
have anything to do with it.**

Epilogue

Final words in this extravaganza of squit – in broad Norfolk, of course!

Here are some proudly local versions of famous quotations. See if you can peel away the coats of Norfolk paint and reveal the originals. Then I'm sure you'll agree they benefit considerably from being given the squit treatment.

1. He say "Less hev some light on the job!" an' thass how it wuz.

2. Thass suffin' rafty up on Mousehold, ole partner!

3. Them warmints! They lay inter them dawgs an' clobbered the cats an' even hed a go at the little ole bearbies in thar cots.

4. Titty-totty, little ole shudderin' warmint, Yew're frit!

5. Dew yew pile pletty o'grub inter that gal Nelly!

6. This here good thing what I'm a'gorn ter dew now, thass the best thing I're ever dun.

7. Yit yew still keep a'standin' on yar hid, dunt yew think yar a bit old fer that?

8. Thass a likeness o' the pearnter when he wunt werry old.

9. Thass that toime o' year when there's a dag abowt an' th'apples are comin' on nicely.

10. I gotter clear orff ter the coost agin, ter where thass wholly quiet. An' orl I want is a big ole boat an' a star so I kin steer har.

11. This here country want evrawun ter do what they hatter do.

A tourist is someone who travels to find things that are different - and then complains when they are.

12. A dickey! A dickey! Orl I're got fer a dickey!

13. Dew yew think, jist cors yew're a'bein' good, there ent gorter be no more cearkes an' beer?

14. I wuz steppin' out orl on m'own when, cor blarst, orl of a sudden, I saw 'em, gret ole loads o' pretty yeller flowers.

15. Fare y'well, ole bewty. That right upset me ter see yew go, but dunt yew worry I'll be abowt fust thing i' the mornin'

16. Clear orff, yew blarsted dawg!

THE ORIGINALS

1. And God said "Let there be light"; and there was light.
   Genesis 1, 3

2. There's a wind upon the heath, brother!
   George Borrow, *Lavengro*

3. Rats! They fought the dogs and killed the cats and bit the babies in their cradles
   The Pied Piper of Hamelin, Robert Browning

4. Wee, sleekit, cow'rin, tim'rous beastie, O what a panic's in thy breastie!
   To a Mouse, Robert Burns

5. Don't let poor Nelly starve!
   Charles II

6. It is a far, far better thing that I do, than I have ever done;
   Sidney Carton, *The Tale of Two Cities,* Charles Dickens

Most husbands want their wives to wear their dresses longer. About two years longer.

7. And yet you incessantly stand on your head - Do you think at your age, it is right?
    Alice in Wonderland, Lewis Carroll.

8. A Portrait of the Artist as a Young Man
    James Joyce

9. Season of mists and mellow fruitfulness
    To Autumn, John Keats

10. I must down to the seas again, to the lonely sea and the sky, And all I want is a tall ship and a star to steer her by.
    Sea Fever, John Masefield

11. England expects every man will do his duty
    Signal at the battle of Trafalgar, Admiral Lord Nelson

12. A horse! A horse! My kingdom for a horse!
    Richard III, William Shakespeare

13. Dost thou think, because thou art virtuous, there shall be no more cakes and ale?
    Sir Toby Belch, *Twelfth Night,* William Shakespeare

14. I wandered lonely as a cloud....when all at once I saw a crowd, a host of golden daffodils.
    William Wordsworth

15. Good night, good night! Parting is such sweet sorrow that I shall say good night till it be morrow.
    Romeo and Juliet, Shakespeare

16. Out, dammed spot, out I say.
    Macbeth, Shakespeare

Education does not change. It's teaching a child how to talk and then teaching it to keep quiet.

Busy on the squit production line… with Major Egbert Gladstone-Pyle as minder.

A perfect window on Skipper's world.

Is an encyclopaedia a system for collecting dust in alphabetical order?